Endorsements

As a parent of a child with Trisomy 18, I found this book to be very much like my life for almost 37 years. I felt the feelings and remembered the many hospital stays. This book shows the need for community support and the way the family became such advocates for their daughter. They taught the medical professionals the pain but mostly the joy that comes with the unconditional love we have for our children.

> Barbara VanHerreweghe
> *SOFT President*
> *Mom to Stacy, 36 years old, Trisomy 18 Angel*

"Walking Her Home" is an honest and open testimony to how this family clung to Jesus as their firm foundation when a severe 'storm' affected them. In many ways, this book is a sad story, but in reality it is a triumphant story of God's love, protection and care for them and for one little girl, Grace, who was such an important part of their family for a few short years. This storm put immense strain on both Cami and Rich, and their marriage, as they tried to balance caring for little Grace while still meeting the needs of their other children. Cami testifies to the fact that because they have made Jesus their firm foundation, He has been there with them in all the storms that have come their way.

> Beverly Lindsay
> *Wolverhampton, England*

Walking Her
Home

Learning to Say, "Your Will, Not Mine"

Cami Lundt

Carpenter's Son Publishing

Published by Carpenter's Son Publishing, Franklin, Tennessee

Editing by Adept Content Solutions

Cover Design and Interior Design by Suzanne Lawing

Printed in the United States of America

978-1-952025-88-4

In loving memory of

Grace Noel Lundt

Your precious life was a miracle and a gift that I will forever treasure. Your life was full of joy and love, and was a witness to so many people that God is good! You were a life-changer for me and many others. You turned our eyes toward Jesus, the lover of our souls, as well as to heaven, where all things will be made new.

Dedicated to

Richard Lundt

Thank you for sticking with me on this journey of life! We have made it through pain and trials, and have come out stronger because of them. Gracie was blessed to have you as her dad. Thank you for your support during the years of this process, and in the adventure to come. I love you and thank God for you each day.

Eric, Ethan, and Megan

Thank you for your love and support throughout this process. Your love for Gracie was unwavering and so sweet to watch as a Mom. She adored each one of you! Spending time with you all gave her the most joy. You all were so helpful and loving to her through all of her medical issues. Instead of being ashamed or embarrassed of her, you chose to be proud. You prayed faithfully for her, and God was so good to answer your prayers. I hope this book might help you remember with joy, but also have some clarity about those five precious years of our family's life, and that you might praise God for His goodness in it. I love you all so much and am so proud of you all.

Family, Friends, and the Body of Believers

Thank you so much for your prayers, support, and love during our years with Gracie. We could not have done it without you. God used each of you to provide our every need over and over. You all cleaned our house multiple times every time we moved, made meals, watched and kept our kids through many hospitalizations, fixed my van, loaned me your vehicle, visited and prayed with us at the hospital, sat with Gracie in the hospital so I could go home and see my family (even on Christmas day), sat with me through surgeries, encouraged me and loved my family well. We are especially grateful to Evangelical Bible Church in Omaha, NE; Bulverde Baptist Church in Bulverde, TX; and Sagebrush Church in Albuquerque, NM. You were all family, when our family could not always be present.

Trisomy 13 children and families

To the children: You are brave warriors who smile even when life is hard and painful. You each are so unique and beautiful. You are a blessing to your family, the medical community, and the world.

To the families: Your bravery and courage inspires me. I have watched you advocate and fight for your children, to give them the best possible life. Most importantly, I have seen you love unconditionally.

To those families who have had to grieve their precious child: I hope this book brings you peace.

Contents

1

Praise You in the Storm

December 12, 2006: "We have some concerns with the brain and the heart. We want you to get a second opinion from a perinatal specialist. The brain ventricles are pushing the normal limits and the heart has some calcification buildup, but often these take care of themselves and dissolve with time."

While I was driving home in my blue minivan that day, these words kept ringing through my head. What could they possibly mean? The doctor had been very vague and brief. He really didn't sound negative, so maybe I could still hope. Then again, how could he put this news any other way? I had gone that day to my first ultrasound of my fourth pregnancy with my three children. Eric was ten, Ethan was eight, and Megan was five. My husband Rich was unable to get away from work for the appointment, but since it was our fourth time around, I had assured him that I would be good! The kids had known we were pregnant for a few months now and were very excited to be having another baby added to our family. I never dreamed that our news would not have been good. I had already had three beautiful, healthy children. We had found out that our baby was a little girl! How perfect could that be? Our family was going to round out to two boys and two girls! A best friend for each of my kids right in our own family!

The doctor was very professional and did his best to tell me the news discreetly without alarming the kids. Eric, though, picked up on a little of it and asked me on the way home what the doctor meant. I answered him vaguely because I honestly did not understand what the doctor had told me. I mentioned only the heart calcifications because I could tell him that those often go away and we just needed to pray for God to heal the baby! I thought that was enough for a ten-year-old to handle. As for me, I fought back tears and clung to the hope that the baby would be okay. I was an avid listener to K-Love radio, and on the way home a song came on that I had never heard before. "Praise You In This Storm" by Casting Crowns seemed to pierce my heart. I was fearful for the life of this sweet baby girl I was carrying, worried about how to protect the three precious children I already had, and anxious about how to tell Rich the news. This was certainly a storm and somehow God was telling me to praise Him! None of it seemed to fit together.

As soon as I got home, I called Rich. We had celebrated our sixteenth wedding anniversary in August and yet I was worried about telling him. I had pushed for this baby, wanting just one more child! He had been ready to be done after our two boys were born so I was really pushing it. I got my girl when Megan was born, so he didn't really think we should tempt fate and try for another. But he finally said yes to make me happy. One of his fears with each pregnancy was that we may have a child with health issues or problems. He had expressed this to me in the past, but I never thought too much of it because it wasn't a fear of mine and I didn't really think that was even a possibility. So to me, it wasn't a fear to think twice about.

Fighting back tears, I told him what the doctor had told me after the ultrasound. He, of course, had many questions about what it could possibly mean, questions that would have been good to ask that I had never even thought to ask. He was always that way, wanting to know the details and intricacies of everything, while having a general idea was always good enough for me. I told him that we would have to wait until we saw the perinatologist to get the answers to the many questions we had. Then I called my family and friends so they could all start praying. I knew they would. I had grown up in a Christian family and accepted Christ as my Savior at the age of eight. Taking our cares and worries to the Lord was just what we had always done, but our cares and worries had always been quite small. My prayer life had stayed very shallow and on the surface. I knew of the acronym for prayer with the word ACTS: Adoration, Confession, Thanksgiving, and Supplication. I always seemed to manage to get the last two parts into my prayer time, the thanksgiving and supplication (requests), but fell short on the adoration and confession. Somehow, I had convinced myself that I was being selfish if I was praying for myself, that my prayers should always focus on the needs of others. Now I desperately needed to pray for this baby and for our family to get through this.

I had grown up in a good old Baptist church that preached the Word of God, and while they didn't necessarily preach legalism and a list of "Do's and Don'ts," I tended to "do" many things because I knew it was what I should be doing. Or I did many things because I thought it would be fun! I grew up on a farm in northwest Iowa that was a mile from the nearest neighbor. Friends were only seen at church, school, or whatever activities I did. So by high school I had become very active in church and school. My faith in Christ was handed down to me from my parents and I believed without question everything the pastor preached, Sunday school teachers taught, and youth leaders put before me. Thankfully it was a very good church that preached from God's Word and built a strong foundation in me. If the church doors were open, we were there. Sunday morning we had Sunday school and church, Sunday evening was youth group and church, youth activities on Wednesday nights, as well as Vacation Bible School, choir practice, and any Bible camps or retreats that were offered.

I was also blessed with a wonderful family that loved the Lord and lived their love for Him in their everyday lives. I knew my grandmothers, both paternal and maternal, prayed for me. Both of my grandfathers were also godly men but had died in my youth. When I called for prayers for my unborn baby, the phones of family and friends started ringing throughout many states, and many people began to pray. I loved the Lord and believed in Him, but until now had never been hit with anything so personal that struck straight to the core of my being. So we prayed and waited for our next appointment.

***

December 21, 2006: The doctor's office had tried to get us to wait until January for the next ultrasound, but we knew we couldn't wait that long. On this day, my friend came to pick up the three kids. Her children were some of my children's best friends and we spent a lot of time together, so no questions were asked as to why we were sending them off to play. Rich and I drove to the ultrasound in an awkward silence. I know we were both fearful of what we might find out. I was worried that Rich would be angry with me or blame me if the news was bad. I hadn't told him that in the first few months of my pregnancy, God had placed some special needs children in my path. It was not like I had never seen or noticed special needs children before, but there is just something different when God tugs at your heart and tells you to pay attention. And it felt to me that somehow that was what He had been doing. I didn't want to be fearful, but it was like God was preparing my heart for what was to come. They were sweet, beautiful, happy children in their preschool years who were incredibly lovable! Yet, I was afraid to tell Rich, not because I thought he would be mean or ugly to me, but because I was afraid of hearing that he had been right and we should not have become pregnant again.

Also on the drive to the hospital, God had that song on the radio again just for me. I remember listening to the words of the song: "I'll praise you in this storm. I will lift my hands. For You are who

You are, no matter where I am. And every tear I've cried, You hold in Your hand. You never left my side. And though my heart is torn, I will praise You in this storm." I remember telling the Lord very specifically that I had no idea what this storm was going to be, but I would do my best to praise Him no matter what. Thankfully the hospital was not too far from our home. We had the ultrasound, and the technician was diligently taking all the measurements and checking every part of our baby's tiny body. She pointed out things as normal and explained what she was measuring, not giving us any indication that anything was wrong. Of course, she was not allowed to tell us that anything wasn't right. From my perspective, the baby looked good. I couldn't tell all the tiny details, but the fuzzy ultrasound image looked like a baby to me! The technician also took all of our medical history. Then we had more waiting until the doctor came in to talk to us about the results. Rich and I talked and held hands. I felt stronger when we were together, even though I was still filled with fear.

The perinatologist came into our room that seemed very cold and dark. I was still on the bed and Rich was standing beside me holding my hand. The doctor pulled up the pictures on the ultrasound screen and started pointing out to us the problems he saw with our little girl. He was kind in giving us the bad news, but he had obviously been the bearer of bad news before because he did not seem to be moved emotionally at all. He showed us how our little girl's cerebellum in her brain was not connected as it should be. He explained that the cerebellum has two parts that should connect to make a figure eight or a peanut shape. Our little girl's cerebellum was split in two halves with fluid in between. He explained that this was called a Dandy-Walker brain malformation, and then proceeded to tell us all the statistics that go along with this problem. He said that it is 65 percent fatal, 65 percent leads to chromosome defects, and 65 percent are born with an IQ of less than 83. He also said that with all of the calcification buildup in our little girl's heart, she probably had a chromosome defect. He explained that she most likely had what he called Trisomy 13 or Trisomy

18. These are two chromosome disorders that most likely would cause a baby to die in utero or, if she made it to birth, to die within no more than five minutes. He urged us to get an amniocentesis so he could tell us more specifically what our baby had.

He also told us that at that hospital they would deliver the baby at twenty-four weeks and that it was called a "premature delivery." I couldn't believe what I was hearing. I knew that was not premature delivery. It was abortion! There were no other words for it. I had spent many early Saturday mornings picketing at the abortion clinic in Omaha, Nebraska, during my years at Grace College of the Bible. There was no doubt in my mind what kind of delivery that would be. If our baby was delivered at twenty-four weeks, she would not stand a chance. There was no question in my mind that I would never even give that option any thought.

The doctor gave Rich and I time to talk to decide what we should do. We knew there were slight risks to doing an amniocentesis but thought that if we knew what our baby had, we could better prepare ourselves and especially our children for what was to come. I had never thought when I first heard about amniocentesis that I would ever do it, due to the risk. I knew it would never change my thoughts on carrying a baby to term or how we thought of the baby, but I had to think of the rest of my family. I had to prepare my children as best I could if we were not going to be able to bring a baby home this time. So the procedure was done. As they did it, I begged and pleaded that God would protect my baby and that it would not hurt her or bring her any more risk at all. I prayed that with my whole heart.

The next twenty-four hours as we waited for the test results, it seemed like there was no possible way for life to be worse. Our fears escalated as we learned more about the Dandy-Walker brain malformation. This could involve possible head enlargement because of the extra fluid on the brain, deafness, blindness, all these chromosome defects, and the list just went on and on. I was not as friendly with the computer as Rich was so I didn't really look on my own. He told me what he found and then I was advised by my mother-in-law to not even look, because the pictures that were online were difficult to see. The kids came back home and were a good distraction. I kept praying and hoping that the news would not be so bad, that these "possible diagnoses" would not become factual.

Then the call came from the doctor on Friday afternoon at about 4:00. I am sure this was not the kind of news the doctor wanted to be telling anyone the Friday before Christmas. The results showed that our little girl had full Trisomy 13, which the doctor explained is "universally fatal." Those were the words that I did not want to hear. *This precious baby growing inside of me would not live.* He went on to tell me more statistics. Not only did our baby have the horrible statistics of the Dandy-Walker brain malformation, but also these: 15 to 25 percent of babies with this chromosome disorder are stillborn; 99.9 percent die in the next few minutes after birth. There was not one statistic told to me of a Trisomy 13 child who had lived, who had beat the odds, or even who had lived for an hour! No hope was given, no hope. The doctor said he would set us up to meet a geneticist, although I was not sure what the purpose of that was to be. The conversation ended quickly after that.

I know that I was in shock, but what questions do you ask when you are given no hope for life? How do you celebrate Christmas when you are out of hope? I had three wonderful children who deserved a wonderful Christmas. I told Rich the results of the test that the doctor had shared with me. We decided we would do Christmas as planned and wait until after we met with the geneticist to tell the kids, which would also be after Christmas. We knew we would need all the prayer we could get in the months to come. I wanted so desperately for God to do a miracle and bring healing to this sweet, precious baby girl inside me. We called almost all our family and friends.

In the midst of making those calls, I called our life insurance representative. Rich and I had always put our children on our policy so if there was ever an unexpected death, it would be covered. We weren't sure if this baby could be put on the policy but thought we should try. Our representative also happened to be a deacon at our church. When I told him what we had learned, he gave words of sympathy and comfort and then said one thing that I will forever remember: "Cami, this was not a surprise to God." Indeed it was not! The God of the universe, who created everything and everyone, had knit this baby together in my womb. This diagnosis was not a surprise to Him.

***

I continued making calls and when I got to my sister-in-law Lisa, my heart ached in a different way. They had lost a precious baby girl in their fourth month of pregnancy a few years ago. They had named her Hannah Faye, and I was one of the blessed ones who was there the day they had to deliver her lifeless body. I saw how precious she was and was able to hold her tiny frail body. I was concerned my news would open up Lisa's old wounds that came with losing her own baby. Instead, Lisa was very sympathetic in my brokenness. By this point, I felt the need to name this baby inside of me. I didn't just want everyone praying for some unknown baby girl! I wanted them to be praying specifically for her by name. Lisa told me that one of the names they considered when they had Hannah was Grace. I thanked her for the idea and then took it straight to Rich. He and I had always named our children together, even though some were easier to agree on than others. We already had an Eric, Ethan, and Megan. So our logical thought process at the beginning of the pregnancy would be for this baby's name, if it were a girl, to begin with the letter "M." We hadn't even really discussed potential names yet since we had just recently learned the baby was a girl, so when I brought the name "Grace" to Rich, he agreed. We thought that the name Grace would be good to remind us of God's gift, and that she was a gift, no matter how long we had her with us. We couldn't think of a middle name at that time, but I was confident God would give us a special one. So I let everyone know that they were now to be praying for Baby Grace.

Another important phone call I made was to the pastor of our church. I wanted our church body to be praying for this baby. I explained everything to Pastor, and then he asked if there were any ladies in the church that I would like him to tell so they could call and talk with me. We had been at the church for five years, and I knew many wonderful ladies there. Two came to mind instantly. One lady was a mom of four, and one of the four kids was special needs. The other lady who came to mind was one that I had watched and listened to, not someone I knew very well at all. Just from watching her, I knew she was a strong woman of faith in the Lord with a sweet, almost quiet spirit. So I asked rather hesitantly, "Do you think your wife would be able to call me?" Pastor of course said yes, he would talk to her.

I am not sure I really expected much to come from that except maybe a phone call or two. In my head, pastors' wives were the friendly faces you saw around church but never those with whom you had much of a close relationship. Boy, was I wrong! Rosi called me quickly, and that relationship became one of the most vital relationships to me during that pregnancy. She became one of the many stones that God placed around me to keep me strong. She was to me like Aaron and Hur were to Moses when the nation of Israel went to battle with Amalek. Moses had to hold up his arms for the Israelites to have victory. The battle went on for so long, Moses became weary and couldn't hold up his arms anymore. That's when Aaron and Hur stepped in and held them up for him. (Exodus 17:12–13). Rosi prayed with me that very first time on the phone and asked if she could meet with me when we got back from our Christmas travels. I eagerly accepted the invitation, knowing that I would need as much support and prayer as possible. She met with me every week to talk and study Scripture. She was so helpful in keeping my focus on God and in answering my doubts about Him that I had never had before. She was someone who could listen to my heart.

On December 23, 2006, I wrote in my journal about the doctor's call and the statistics he had given us. I ended that entry with this:

It sounds like our baby girl gets to go see God's glory soon.

Psalm 121:1–2, "I will lift up my eyes to the hills—where does my help come from? My help comes from the Lord, the Maker of heaven and earth."

Deut. 31:6, "Be strong and courageous. Do not be afraid or terrified because of them, for the Lord your God goes with you; he will never leave you nor forsake you."

I am very afraid and unsure of what the next four months will bring, but I know that my God will be with me for it all. My prayer is that Richard, and the kids, and I, and all those around us will lean totally on Christ and our faith will grow stronger through it all. Lord, I desire for you to receive all praise and glory from whatever is to come.

We celebrated Christmas with our children the next morning and then headed to my parents' home in Iowa to celebrate Christmas with the family. Thankfully the trip to the farm was only an hour and a half long. Christmas was still fun for the kids. They love being at the farm and spending time with their cousins. There is always plenty to do, outside and in! It was rather emotional for me, because with each family member came the conversation about what the doctor had said. So the normal joys that came with being pregnant were now turned to sorrow. It was still a blessing for me to share with them because my family is full of strong believers, so prayers and encouragement along with comfort were very present. We were also blessed to spend time with Rich's parents who also comforted and encouraged us. I felt strengthened by the army of believers around me, knowing that the prayer warriors were stepping into battle with me. Even so, it was the worst Christmas of my life, pretending with my children that I was happy and all was well and knowing in my heart the truth.

While at the farm for Christmas, we went to church on that Sunday. For some reason Dad rode with me and the kids. I was playing the *Christmas Shoes* CD as it had become our favorite Christmas CD. I loved the many songs that told life stories and the kids loved "The Grinch." The song "Sing Noel" came on, and at that moment I knew that "Noel" would be the middle name of our little girl. I just started crying because I knew it was an answer to my prayer. Immediately after church I went to the bookstore to find out the meaning of the name. The book said that Noel meant Christmas child and precious gift. Grace Noel was the perfect name. She was not a Christmas baby, not conceived then or going to be born at Christmas time, yet I knew she would help point people to the real Christmas child, Jesus.

***

I was thankful that Rich had also been able to talk to some of his Christian brothers. He had questions and concerns and was very worried about what the outcome would be. I prayed that God would continue to give him brothers in Christ to share with, seek advice from, and to lean on. He shared with me that he felt like we were going to have this big dark cloud over us until the baby died. He didn't want that for our family. While I heard him and understood that men and women think very differently, I was feeling the total opposite. With Christmas right in front of me, and the story of Jesus's birth in my thoughts again, I was reminded of how Mary had not had a normal pregnancy. She was a betrothed virgin and could have been stoned to death or put away. There was nothing simple and easy about that pregnancy, yet God had specifically chosen her to be the mother of Jesus, the Savior of the world! Quite quickly after our diagnosis I realized that I, like Mary, was specifically chosen by God to be Grace's mommy! I was the one that He had chosen. He picked me out of all the women in the world to carry her in my womb. I knew that God doesn't give you anything that He doesn't also give you the strength to handle. I felt honored and privileged. I did not feel a dark cloud over me. Yes, there would be days and moments of intense sadness and grief, but fear of those moments was not the prevailing feeling in me. I felt it was a privilege to be Grace's mommy, even if she was just in my

21

womb for a short time. Even if I was never to hold her physical living body that could hear and feel me, to see her breathe or smile, or hear her cry, I wanted to enjoy every moment of that pregnancy! I wanted to speak loving words to her and rub on her lovingly. I wanted her to know that she was loved and wanted. She had started kicking early in the pregnancy, and she didn't just move and kick a little bit, she kicked a lot! I had been pregnant three times before, and she seemed so much more active than any of my other babies. It was such a blessing and reassurance to me that she was alive and active. Every time she kicked, I would rub my tummy where she kicked and tell her how much I loved her!

It was hard getting back into school and church activities after the Christmas break, because that meant I had to come face to face with many people, and the truth of my heartache was not easy to conceal. So I did the best I could, especially in front of my kids and Rich. There were other times when I was alone that I didn't even try. When asked how I was or how I was feeling, the truth came out along with many tears. I was thankful for so many caring people who were praying for us and for the baby.

We told the children the diagnosis after the geneticist appointment. They all took it really hard and didn't understand. It wasn't easy for us to understand completely, so how could we help a ten-, eight-, and five-year-old understand?

Rich hadn't said much lately. Earlier, he told me that he thought I was carrying enough emotion and didn't want to add to it. He said he felt a heavy heart from me all the time. I thought I had faked it better than that. As I thought about it, I thought that probably explained why the boys and Megan had been hugging me so much more lately. At bedtime one night, I asked the boys why all the hugs lately. Eric said, "I don't know why." Ethan said, "I just don't want you being so sad about the baby." While it was true I was sad, I also had a lot of fear about the decisions that we would have to make when the baby was born.

The doctors had both pushed "comfort care." Comfort care is when you don't take any extreme measures to help the baby live, you simply keep them comfortable until they die. Rich and I had many conversations about this. He felt strongly that this was what we needed to do, and even though I agreed with him many times over, he thought I would change my mind once the baby was born. Honestly, I had made my decision to follow his lead in this area even though I felt it might tear my heart out to actually do it. I was more concerned that I would hold it against him and not be able to forgive him if my heart wanted something else when it came to the actual moment. He also told me that he found himself hoping that I would miscarry each day. That hit me hard realizing that it could happen any day. Tomorrow was not guaranteed. I did not want this at all, but I could not be angry with Rich for telling me how he felt. I knew he was just desiring to protect his family and get the pain and grief over so we could move on with our lives. However I told him that I felt like each day I carried her in my womb was another day that she could get stronger and God could do a miracle! I was counting on that miracle!

I was thankful at the time that we could be honest with each other and still love each other, but looking back on those days I see how Satan was using this pregnancy to divide us. I found myself going to my friends and family for the support I needed. Rich clung to our other three children and took a lot of his pain on himself by withdrawing from me. I didn't realize how divided we had become until much later on in our marriage. Our house at that time was a split level, and I do specifically remember how I would suffer in silence in the living room on the upper level and he would suffer in silence in the family room on the lower level. The kitchen was our middle ground, but togetherness in our suffering was not something we did much at all for the next few months. I know that much of this was my fault.

I had come to depend on my friends and family in my time of crisis. I called them when I needed to talk. I cried to them when my hurt was unbearable. I should have been going to Rich for comfort and strength, but I went elsewhere, leaving him alone. The people I was going to were not bad in any way. They were people who I knew would pray and encourage me in the Lord. I didn't realize at the time that this crisis would either bring Rich and me closer together or cause division. Unfortunately, it was the latter. The crisis was having a huge effect on our marriage, which definitely was not just staying the same. Rich and I were learning to do life separately.

***

We had been married in 1990 after I graduated from college. Rich had graduated in 1991. I worked hard as an elementary education teacher at three different Christian schools in the Omaha/Council Bluffs area for the six years of our marriage before we decided to start our family. Eric was born August 27, 1996. Rich had started as a bellman at the Red Lion Hotel in college and had become the Guest Services Manager at the hotel soon after we were married. He graduated with a business degree and started working his way up in the hotel business. He was a very hard worker and soon became the Front Desk Manager, and then worked his way into the Sales Office. He switched over to a different hotel in Omaha where he fine-tuned his skills and broadened his knowledge. Exactly two years after our first son was born, our second son was born! Yes, it was the same day and no, it wasn't planned by anyone but God himself! A year after our second son was born, Rich had his first opportunity to be General Manager of a hotel. That sounded wonderful, except for the fact that it was in Rio Rancho, New Mexico. With two little ones, we enjoyed living close to family and had many friends in the Omaha area. This was a big decision for our family to make. Rich felt strongly that it would be a great opportunity for his career, and I knew that it was my job to support him. I had stopped teaching when Eric was born and was just doing some daycare in our home at the time. We truly needed to live off Rich's salary if I was to stay home with the boys. So off we went to the desert in March of 1999!

We knew absolutely no one there. We had never even visited or vacationed there. Even though it was hard to leave everyone, I did feel an incredible peace that God was in control and all would be well. We bought a house in Rio Rancho and quickly fell in love with everyone and everything about New Mexico! We loved the mountains, the weather, our home, the church we found, and the employees at Rich's hotel. It was also at this time in New Mexico that I found the Christian radio station K-Love and totally fell in love with the encouraging words and songs that they offered. Friendships were coming along and everyone there was very welcoming. Unfortunately we didn't get to stay there very long. God had other plans. A few months after we arrived, Rich's hotel was sold to another company! Rich explained our choice to me this way: "We can either stay here and hope that this new company likes me, or we can move to another hotel that the company who hired me owns." It made sense to us both that it would be safer to stay with the company that had hired him, so in August of 2000 we sold our home and moved to Wichita, Kansas. As we drove away from Rio Rancho, New Mexico, I remember telling God that I would love to come back to that place someday. It didn't seem like a very feasible place to go for vacation or a visit, but God placed that desire in my heart for a very specific purpose that I wouldn't realize until almost eleven years later.

Describing our experience at Wichita, Kansas, is a little more difficult. While the hotel was a good hotel and Rich did very well there, this place was not our dream place to live. Maybe it was because we had loved New Mexico. We were renting a home as we'd not lived in our New Mexico home long enough to make any money on the sale. The home and neighborhood were very nice, but we had a difficult time finding a church body. Once we finally did settle on one, it was incredibly hard to feel welcome or like we fit in. In New Mexico the ladies had been so quick to welcome me and fit me into their lives with play dates and coffee. I hadn't to do anything but say yes! After a couple months, I realized this was not going to happen in Wichita. I remember sitting through some church services alone when Rich had to work on Sundays, just crying because I felt so alone. One night as I was helping at church, I decided that I was going to need to be the one to make the first move.

I am not saying that Wichita is a horrible place where no one can ever make friends. I came to realize that New Mexico was a place of transplants, where most everyone was from somewhere else. They all knew what it was like to be the new person in town so they were very quick to welcome the new person. Wichita, however, was not like that at all. Almost everyone I met had been born and raised there. They all had family and friends there with whom they did everything. They didn't reach out to make the new friend because they didn't need the new friend or possibly even have time for a new friend. I realize this was not true for everyone, but it sure seemed the reality for me.

By now I had become involved in the Cubbies program where my boys were on Wednesday night. I was highly experienced with this from my previous church in Omaha, so I became one of the many helpers. One evening I noticed another little boy about Eric's age and realized that his mother was helping also. So I introduced myself and started a conversation with her. She had an accent that I was not familiar with at all. Apparently, she was from Israel and had lived in Canada also. Now she and her family of five lived in Wichita. It wasn't long before I invited her and her children over to my home for a play date! We soon became good friends, as we both had no others, it seemed. Thankfully, Wichita also had K-Love, so I was able to still be encouraged and fed through their music as well as at church.

While in Wichita, we were blessed to get pregnant once again. Once again we were due in August. A few months before our first little girl was born, Rich was off to Omaha, Nebraska, for another job change. We were eager to leave Wichita, and Omaha was already like home. Being close to family and friends made this a very easy decision. Rich would be opening a hotel for his company in Omaha. This would be a challenge for him as he had never opened a hotel before, but it would also be a great learning experience for his professional career. Rich had to go a couple months ahead of us. I would stay back and finish out the pregnancy with the doctor who had been following me. We had never scheduled a "birth" day for any of our children but decided that was needed for this time around so that we could be sure that Rich would be home for the birth of our baby girl. Megan was born on August 3, 2001. We stayed in Wichita for two more weeks before we moved the family to Omaha.

Anyone who knows me is aware that I am always trying to figure out "why" God does what He does, especially if it appears that we are going in circles! So I did not understand why our stays in New Mexico and Kansas were so short or why we would be going back to Nebraska. I came to the conclusion that God wanted us there to be close to our family for someone that may need our help, perhaps an illness or a death. That seemed the most logical reason to me. We would be there to support and help the family when the time of need came. I did not realize at the time that God was bringing us back because we would need the support and the help of our own family.

Moving back to Omaha was a fun move! We now had three beautiful children who could easily be loved on by many family members and friends. I had all my old dear friendships to fall back on as well as new ones that God had brought into my life. I remember questioning God about one of the new friendships, wondering *Why has He brought me into her life?* I thought I had absolutely nothing to offer her and no way to support her in her time of need. Her situation was completely foreign to me. Yet God would develop that friendship into such a sweet and dear friendship that would prove to be vital in my future as well.

We stepped back into our church as if we had never been gone. We had frequent visits from grandparents and were always able to spend holidays with family. I loved all of this! The hard part was that opening a new hotel was very intense and time consuming. Rich had always had a strong work ethic so he would do whatever it took to make sure that hotel succeeded. Unfortunately, the hotel was a bit of a drive from our home so the visits the kids and I had been able to make to his hotels in New Mexico and Kansas to have breakfast, go for a swim, and see Daddy did not happen any more in Omaha. With his long hours, we did not get much time with him.

After a few years at this hotel, Rich transferred to a hotel closer to our home. By then the boys were in school and I was out of the habit of making the hotel visits a priority. His hours were better, but our time was really starting to focus on our kids. Both boys were in football, basketball, and baseball. Every once in a while, Rich would express his concern to me that he did not want to be one of those couples who have nothing in common once the kids were gone. I would always assure him that would not be us! After all, we had a few things in common! We both liked the Huskers, had some "couple friends" who matched up for us together, and would always love our kids and eventually grandkids. I never seemed to calculate the many things we did separately or the things we did together. If I had calculated that against our common interests, I would have realized that we were out of balance. However, I was quite content to keep trudging through life as it was. Yes, I tried to be a good wife. I thought I was putting him first after my Lord. I thought I was serving him well. I thought I was loving him well. I thought that was enough. I honestly didn't get much fulfillment out of our relationship. I was fulfilled by mothering our children and also by my relationships with my friends. Even the time I gave to good activities at church or school seemed to take priority. Rich would agree to everything I asked to do and I said yes to everything he asked to do. I didn't realize then that we were consenting to the division of our marriage with every "yes" we gave.

Time marched on as the kids grew. I babysat for a friend for some extra cash, and then took a part-time job at the YMCA working with preschool kids so Megan could go with me. After a few years I started getting the itch for just one more baby. Rich was resistant at first and I wore him down once again. I had come from a family of four kids and that seemed about perfect to me. He had come from a family of six kids, so I didn't understand why he wouldn't want more! Of course, I just thought about the sweet cuddly baby to love once again. He thought in terms of how many mouths to feed, and he worried whether another child would be born healthy. When we moved back to Omaha, I was delighted that K-Love had come to this city in the time that we had been gone. So once again I was loving my Christian music. Life was good!

***

Now here we were in the middle of a very difficult pregnancy. There were many hard and heavy-hearted days. On Ethan's 100th day of school that they celebrated, he had written in his school journal that he dedicated the book to his baby sister. When I saw it and called him to me, I told him how sweet it was to have done that. He just burst into tears and cried and cried. My heart broke for my sweet little boy. The next day they wrote in their journals about chapel and he wrote a prayer asking Jesus to make his baby sister better and to help her not to die. He was only eight. I tried so hard to point the kids to Jesus through the pregnancy. We prayed and prayed for Jesus to heal Grace and do a miracle. No matter what the doctors said, I knew God could do it!

Many of my hardest moments were seeing other mothers with babies, especially newborns. It seemed they were all over, at work, at church, at school. God was so sweet in His love for me through the pregnancy. He knew I was hurting and He encouraged me through Scripture, through the body of believers, through giving me hope to keep praying and trusting in Him. Many times it was an encouraging word from a friend, a meal brought by someone from the church, a song on the radio.

One day as I was driving, a song came on that I had heard many times. It was a sweet song by Mark Schultz that told of a love story. It told of a couple's first date, the day they had a child, and the time of his wife's death and how he, the husband, was there through it all with her, clear to the end. He was, as the title said, "Walking Her Home." I had always thought it was sweet, though I was not sure if it was a true picture of Rich and me or not. Yet it seemed like the dream marriage every girl wanted. On this day when I listened to it, God gave it a new meaning just for me. The man in that song had been there for his wife through her whole life. He had walked her home from their first date. He had walked her through every joy and sorrow in their life together. Most importantly, he had walked her home to Jesus in heaven, not just on the night she passed away, but through her life. To heaven, our true home and final destination. Through all of our moves, I had learned not to become too attached to a specific home. Each home we had was special in different ways, but none of them were ours for the keeping or staying. While one home had an awesome backyard with beautiful green grass and room to run, climb trees, and sled, the next home had a big kitchen with more cabinets than I needed and a beautiful backyard filled with rocks. We quickly decided on the "need to have" list for every home and it really was rather small. I had come to know that everything here is just temporary. Heaven is our real home, just as God is our Father.

As the song played that day, God revealed to me that I was walking Grace home, home to heaven. I was not sure how short or how long our walk would be. I didn't know if it would be smooth or rocky. Would it be on a straight path where I knew every step of the way or a winding difficult path where I couldn't even see very well? Would I be able to carry the load that I was being asked to carry, or would I need to be carried? Would I be able to be a good wife and mother to my other three children on this walk? All I knew was what the doctors had told me to expect, and I knew that would end up in heartache and despair if I chose to believe them. For me, at that moment, I knew that God had given me this job, this walk. I knew it would not be easy at all. It was by far the most difficult and scary job that I had ever encountered in my life. I had never done anything like it and I didn't know if I was equipped to handle what was to come, but I knew it was a privilege and an honor to be chosen by God to do it. That was a very special day.

I continued to meet with Pastor's wife Rosi and Malinda, mother of two and once again in a high-risk pregnancy. The three of us had a blessed time together as we went through Scriptures that talked about the character of God. We shared our joys, our fears, and our tears. I remember one week as Rosi asked me which character trait we should look at, I just laid it out there honestly with tears that my struggle at that point was that if God was truly my friend, then how could He do this to my baby, to my family, and to me? The two just didn't seem to match up to me at all. This was a very critical time in my life for my faith. I had always accepted everything that I had been taught and studied. I had graduated from Bible college. I had taught at Christian elementary schools. Some might call me too accepting or naïve to believe so easily without challenging or questioning. Now, at the age of thirty-eight, I was questioning the character of the God I had always believed in. I don't know if I was testing Him to see if He really was the God I had grown up believing He was, or if He was testing me to see if my faith in Him would hold fast when something tough came my way. The Scriptures we shared together confirmed my faith in my God, and my friend. I knew that "His ways are higher than my ways, His thoughts higher than my thoughts" (Isa. 55:8–9, paraphrased). I would never totally have all the answers to my questions until I reached heaven myself, and even if I had the answers, I probably still wouldn't like the plan. This is where my faith just had to take over. I knew God loved me so much that He sacrificed His Son for me. What would I be willing to sacrifice?

I also learned a great deal just by being with Malinda. The amazing thing to me was that this was her eighth pregnancy! Three of the pregnancies had been miscarriages. Three others had resulted in her water breaking very early in the pregnancy, one as early as fourteen weeks. That child had lived and was doing well. She had only had one healthy pregnancy. I was amazed that she could go through that loss and pain so many times and still trust that God would help her through this pregnancy! I remember sharing with her that it was hard giving up the hopes and dreams that I had for my baby. Hopes and dreams of seeing my baby grow, learn to walk, play with her siblings, go to school, and the list just went on and on it seemed, all the many things that we sometimes take for granted with our children, because they just happen. Even if my baby survived for only a short time, those things would never happen. Malinda shared with me that her goal through each pregnancy was to have a "surrendered hope." In other words, it was okay for me to have my hopes and dreams for a future with my baby, but I must surrender those hopes over to Christ, realizing that His hopes and dreams and His purpose for Grace are far better. It was with those words of wisdom that I was able to ask God for a miracle and yet accept that His perfect plan for Grace would be best because it was His plan. She was His child to have and to hold forever. The last months of my pregnancy became more difficult when Malinda lost her baby. She was four weeks behind me in her pregnancy. They had kept her on bed rest for as long as they could and they could not hold back the delivery any longer. That was very difficult, because in my head and heart I was sure that God would choose her baby to live this time and that He would take mine home to be with Him. Here I was now, trying to comfort and console her as she continued to love and support and encourage me. She was such a strong woman in the Lord and a wonderful example for me to walk with and learn from.

I continued working at the YMCA part time throughout my pregnancy. I also continued helping in my kids' classes at school and with the kids' program at our church on Wednesday nights. I continued doing all those wife/mom things that we all just do! Sometimes those things were good distractions, but other times they were just hard. Do you know how hard it is to walk past the baby section in Walmart when you know your baby won't live to need any of it? The longing to use diapers and wipes and buy those adorable little girl clothes? I learned to avoid the section as best as I could to try to avoid the tears at the store. There is no easy path in life, though, to avoid all of the pregnant moms with healthy babies growing inside of them or the babies that go past you in the grocery stores, at church, or even on a walk in your neighborhood. All of these things just make you desire and want that baby more. Every time I passed a baby, I found myself thinking the same two words, healthy baby. It was a constant reminder that those babies were healthy and mine was not. Some days were strong days where I could keep my chin held high and a smile on my face and other days my heart was so heavy I felt like I couldn't even breathe. One night I went scrapbooking with my sister to a friend's house. I got about six pages done in my son's album and then at about 10:00 pm I started having some kind of panic or anxiety attack. This had never happened to me before. I had realized that most nights around that time Grace would start to get busy and do her moving around. I tried to keep working, but my focus was totally on the fact that she should be moving and I couldn't feel her. I broke down crying and told my sister that we had to go. Of course, as soon as I got home and was sitting peacefully by Rich at about 11:00 pm., she started moving! Thank you, Lord!

At about thirty-seven weeks, I went in for my checkup and they found that my blood pressure was too high. Their answer for that was for me to go on bed rest. They offered to deliver Grace early, but that just wasn't an option to me. This baby was still alive and well as long as she stayed in me, it appeared! She moved and kicked, did ripple waves across my belly! Every day, every minute she was in me, she was getting stronger and God was still working His miracle. I was not going to rush her to delivery. I was already feeling like the clock was ticking way too fast and that my time with her was coming to an end. I didn't want it to end. If I could have stayed pregnant indefinitely, I would have! As it was I went on bed rest. I cried to my pastor's wife that this just was not possible. My husband worked many hours, didn't cook, and I had three other children to take care of, plus a house! The church had been so good to us. How could I ask them for anything more? She sweetly replied to me, "Cami, you didn't choose this for us, God did." She explained to me how it was the church's job to take care of and minister to the needy and the hurting. God gave this "bed rest" not just to me, but to our church. They and other friends ministered to our family during that time. They provided meals, cleaned my house, did laundry, drove my kids to school and to their practices. Good friends came and spent extra time with me at home helping tend to my children and home. I even had a couple friends come and give me a soothing pedicure. Most importantly, they all continued to pray. They listened to my hurting heart and prayed for our family and for God to miraculously heal this precious baby!

I was incredibly grateful for all those friends, family, and church family. God was so faithful to take care of our whole family during that time. We made it through the next two doctor's visits with flying colors for our little girl. At my thirty-nine-week visit, the doctor said that,

with my blood pressure concerns, he would not let me go past my due date. He wanted to induce me on April 11. I agonized over this decision. God had brought us this far and I didn't like the idea that now we were going to start calling the shots. Unfortunately though, I had always been a fairly obedient and respectful girl. I was not one to speak up or speak out against another person's wishes, so I didn't object. I did, however, take it straight to the Lord. I prayed that God would still do this on His timing. I did not want to be induced so I prayed and prayed that He would bring Grace before the doctor's appointed time.

2

How Can I Keep From Singing?

April 10, 2007 – Grace's due date. We had a good night of rest the night before but as I woke up that morning, my contractions started; I was going into labor. I quickly woke up Rich and the kids and called both sets of parents, my closest friends, the people to call the prayer chain at church, and my dear friend Robin who had planned to come and get the kids to watch them. She came, gave me a hug for comfort and courage, and took the kids to play with hers for the day. Rich and I had a quiet drive to the hospital, reviewed our plan for comfort care, and tried to draw strength from each other.

We arrived at the hospital quickly and they put us in a labor and delivery room with a plaque that said Peace on the door. They gave me a nurse who was a bit older and definitely wise and very tender. She was very comforting and compassionate as she learned of our situation. They had put the call in to my OB-GYN, who had told them to give me Pitocin to get things moving. I panicked right away. That is what I had been given to induce my labor with Megan five years before. It had made my contractions incredibly hard. I did not want that for Grace. I didn't need her to come out quickly and I definitely did not want anything being harder on her. I expressed my concern to the nurse, and she smiled at me and said, "That's okay, we will just take our time doing all of our other prep work and that will be the last thing we do." So that is what she did. She put the monitors on me, took my vital signs, made sure we were comfortable, and took her time.

During this time frame, I didn't realize it, but the lobby was filling up with people who were there for us. They were praying for us and they were just there: Pastor and his wife Rosi, my good friends Cheryl and Malinda, my sister, my mother and father, who had driven the hour and a half as soon as they heard the news, and my grandmother from over two hours away who also wanted to be there, so my aunt had driven her in. We even were blessed to have a photographer from the organization "Now I Lay Me Down to Sleep" there. She happened to be a good friend of my brother-in-law and his wife from their church. My mother-in-law was teaching that day, but she got away as quickly as she possibly could and drove from South Dakota.

I continued laboring rather easily. I wasn't really stressed or anxious. I felt strong and knew that God was in control. I didn't realize that they were not monitoring the baby at all, otherwise I may have wanted to change that. My blood pressure started going up after a while, and the nurse came in to say that the doctor wanted me on the Pitocin. I started to panic, but then remembered a verse that the ladies and I had gone over in the previous weeks about man not being able to change God's plans. I couldn't remember exactly what it was, so I asked the nurse to let Malinda, Rosi, and my mom in to read that verse with me. She did and they came in with their Bibles to read the Scripture and prayed with me. Psalm 56:3–4, "When I am afraid, I will trust in you. In God, whose word I praise, in God I trust; I will not be afraid. What can mortal man do to me?" Psalm 56:10–11, "In God, whose word I praise, in the Lord, whose word I praise—in God I trust; I will not be afraid. What can man do to me?" This Scripture gave me the peace I needed. It reassured my heart once again that nothing man, or the doctors, would do could possibly change the outcome of what God had already planned for my precious baby. God had the plans all laid out and it would happen according to His will. So the Pitocin was given to me, and it did speed things along. Before I knew it, the doctor was in the room asking me to push. Rich was by my side holding my hand through it all. It did not take very many pushes at all before our baby girl arrived. She was alive!

I didn't know at the time, but my best friend Cheryl had been waiting just outside the door of our room. She was updating everyone in the lobby on our status as she heard it through the door! She ran to tell them when it was time to push, and she ran to tell them when Grace let out her first cry! How thankful I am for all of those people and the many others not there who I know were lifting us up in prayer throughout that time. The friends and family who were there rejoiced with us, praising God for His faithfulness. I learned much later on this journey that when God calls the body of Christ to suffer alongside us, to minister to us, to meet our needs, the exciting part is that they also get to enjoy the victory that Jesus gives. That victory that day was not just for Rich and me and our little family. It was for the whole team, the body of believers He had so carefully placed around us. What a sweet victory to share together! He knew exactly what He was doing when He moved us back to Omaha five years before. It was for "such a time as this." Just as Esther was appointed in the Bible to be Queen for "such a time as this." You see, the incredible thing about God is that He sees the end from the beginning. He knows exactly who we need to be near, who will be best to minister to us and help us through our difficult times. We don't have to suffer and hurt alone. He did just that for our family. He saw the need that was coming and positioned us in the right place for it.

What a blessed time to have the doctor put that sweet little baby in my arms. Rich and I were amazed! We both held her, treasuring every second. If only we could pause time and make it last so much longer.

From the reading we had done, we had learned that these Trisomy babies have many different anomalies. An anomaly is a marked deviation from normal, especially as a result of congenital or hereditary defects. Another definition of a developmental anomaly is a structural abnormality of any type present at birth, or a defect resulting from imperfect embryonic development. We had read that many of the Trisomy kids had extra fingers or toes. Many had heart issues. There were many possible visible signs. One of my many prayers for this precious little baby was that God would make her in a way that would not be too difficult for my children to look at her and love her. I knew her time was to be short, and I wanted them to be able to love her without fear of what she looked like. Of course, the Mommy in me also tried to be prepared to help with this as well. I had brought a little pair of baby mittens, booties, and a little pink hat just in case. But none of this was needed, God had answered my prayer with abundance. Grace Noel was absolutely beautiful. There were no extra digits on her hands or feet. Her head had a tiny little hole at the back that you couldn't see with all of her beautiful hair unless you looked really closely. She did not even have a cleft palate lip as many of the Trisomy children had. She did have very adorable toes that were joined a little differently. The only obvious difference was that she did not open her eyes like every "normal" newborn does.

The time spent holding her was so precious. Soon after she arrived the photographer from the organization "Now I Lay Me Down to Sleep" came in and captured so much of everything and everyone on film. We were grateful to have her there because we were still thinking that our time together was going to be brief. Rich helped the nurse give Grace a bath. Oh, how Grace hated the bath. She cried and cried until they ran her head under the faucet to wash her hair. Then the crying stopped and she loved it.

We quickly had everyone from the lobby come in small groups to see her. The three words that kept coming to me later as I reflected on the emotions of that day were *peace, strength,* and *joy*. God had definitely given me a spirit of peace throughout the whole delivery. I was not fearful of what may happen. It was the peace of knowing that

God was in control and that He was the One who had pre-planned the day. Nothing was going to happen by chance. What Rich and I had decided to do or not to do would not change His plan. God had already planned it. I also felt great strength that day. The fears that I had during the pregnancy of wanting to change the plan of comfort care at the last moment or feeling the desire to intervene with medical help were not there at all. Grace appeared to be holding her own in every respect. I had told God those fears so many times. I had specifically told Him over and over that we were only doing comfort care and that He would need to come through for Grace if she were to live. Thankfully He did!

I was overwhelmed with the complete joy of holding her and seeing her alive, being able to whisper to her how much I loved her and how much we wanted her. I watched Rich hold her with love and tears in his eyes. When our kids came in, I could see that they were all very timid and afraid. We tried to reassure them that it was good for them to hold her. The boys both noticed that her eyes weren't opening and asked about it right away. Tears came as they realized she could not see. They still held her as if she were the most precious thing they had ever seen. Megan was only five years old and couldn't wait to hold her baby sister. She didn't realize until the next day that Grace couldn't see. She just thought she was sleeping. Watching Rich hold her, my kids hold her, and the other family and friends hold her, I could see fear in some eyes. It seemed they were afraid to love completely because Grace could be gone so soon. I could also see the love and amazement in many eyes at the beautiful miracle in their arms. As much as we all longed for that miracle, I am not sure any of us were really expecting it. Now that she was here, how long would she stay? How soon before our hearts would be breaking? The doctors had told us we might expect about five minutes before she passed away. I had prayed for at least fifteen, and hopefully so much more. God answered our prayers in abundance!

After about an hour, our room had really filled up. The family and friends who had been there from the beginning were in our room. I am not sure what the hospital policy was, but I am quite sure we were being allowed to not follow it! Rich's mom had been able to get away from the school where she taught and she had driven the three hours to get there. The word had spread past the walls of the hospital, because so many more people just kept pouring in. They all came hoping to see our little miracle, to hold her, and to share in the joy.

Then, with all of these people in our room, the nurse stepped in and asked me who our pediatrician was. I looked at her in amazement and told her, "We were told we wouldn't need one, so I don't have one." This was completely true! I had asked several doctors and they had all given me the same advice: there was no need for one. The nurse smiled at me and calmly said that she would get one for us. That was another God-ordained and planned part of this whole journey. The doctor they brought was a pediatrician who had her offices in the connecting building to the hospital. She soon came over to meet us and do her newborn exam. She turned out to be an excellent pediatrician who would be so understanding, supportive, and compassionate as she helped us navigate through that first year of Grace's life. What a blessing. I don't think I could have found or picked a better doctor for our little sweetheart.

After some time passed, many of the friends and church family left the hospital. The grandmothers took our children back to the house to watch them and stay for as long as we needed. The photographer had taken some very precious pictures of our little miracle and then left as well. Rich stayed with me and the baby at the hospital. Even though Grace appeared to be doing well, we still expected to lose her at any time. We were still planning on doing comfort care only, although the longer she lived Rich thought that I would change my mind when the time actually came. I knew I needed to stick with the plan that we had chosen, but for now I was just going to treasure each moment we had and try not to worry about what was still coming.

Night came and, as tired as we were, neither one of us wanted to go to sleep. Grace was in the little bed next to mine. We tried to nurse but did not have much success. We finally decided it was time to try to get some sleep. So into the bed she went on her back as was the standard practice of all hospitals at the time. Rich and I were both listening to her every breath, so afraid that one of them would be her last. She did seem to struggle with her breathing so Rich just decided to hold her through most of the night. I was exhausted from giving birth and the many emotions of the day so I got more sleep than he did. We were both very thankful when the sun rose for the new day. Grace had made it through her first night!

With the new day came an ECHO test on Grace's heart, meeting with the lactation consultant to try to get help with breastfeeding Grace, and then the doctor's visit, nurse visit, and a visit from the hospice company. We had not planned on bringing a baby home and now they were talking of sending us all home. I had no idea that hospice companies provided services to little newborns. That was something I had never experienced or seen. I had absolutely no experience with hospice. They were very kind and explained their many services that would benefit our family and Grace. During my other three pregnancies, I had carefully planned and prepared for bringing a new baby home. We had painted and wallpapered nurseries, bought a crib, diapers, clothes—all of the necessities and non-necessities that go along with the joy of bringing a baby home. I had not done any of that for this baby. I had bought one sleeper and one newborn dress in early December to have under the Christmas tree for the new baby that would be joining our family, but when Christmas came I didn't even actually wrap them. By the end of my pregnancy, I thought the dress would be what we would bury our baby in.

That second day in the hospital I called my friend, Cheryl, and told her that I thought we would be bringing Grace home the next day and that we had nothing for her. There were no diapers, wipes, crib, or bassinet. We hadn't even brought our old car seat to the hospital and now we'd need that. Cheryl said not to worry, that she would take care of it. I was able to focus on this precious baby.

That night we did not leave Grace on her back for very long before we decided to try her side. It worked much better! Grace did not seem to struggle with her breathing like the night before. Rich, Grace, and I all slept much more peacefully that night. We woke to the sunrise, a new day, and prepared to go home.

We were told that Grace's heart had looked good from the test the day before. What wonderful news! We had our last consults with the doctors and hospice. They said that she could die from an apnea episode or from failure to thrive, and that the brain condition would eventually make things very difficult as well, either requiring surgery with a shunt put in to drain off fluid or letting it take her life. It was obviously still their opinion that we would not have our little girl too long. Regardless of what they told us and the fact that we were going home only to have her on hospice care, I was still very hopeful and filled with joy. Our little Grace had already lived longer than they said she would. She was a miracle and we were blessed. Cheryl had brought the car seat that we had used for each child. Unfortunately I didn't know that car seats were checked over by the hospital and ours did not meet the new standards. Thankfully the hospital was able to give us a car seat as well as other supplies and gifts, including a beautiful christening gown and much more.

Regardless of the grim prognosis that we were still receiving, it was a very joyful and emotional exit that day from the hospital. My heart was heavy with the emotions, full of fear and yet still full of joy and excitement. God had answered our prayers! How incredibly blessed and thankful we were. Yes, there were tears in my eyes. But Grace Noel was coming home! She would be greeted by three very excited siblings and two very thankful grandmothers. We arrived home to a beautiful white bassinet in the living room. It was surrounded with all of the necessities that we would need. Cheryl had really come through and we were all set to take care of this new little one, or at least we thought we were ready.

Praying family and friends in waiting room

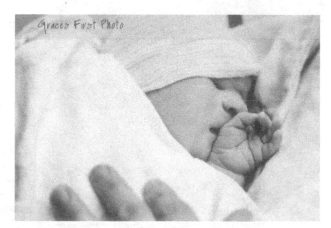

First Photo

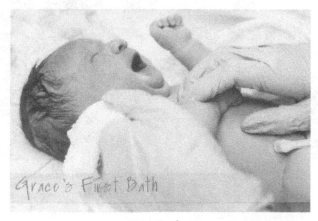

First Bath

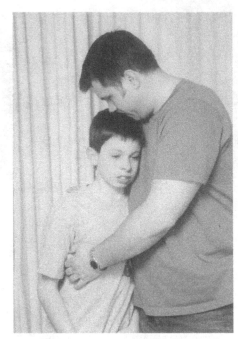

Eric and Rich

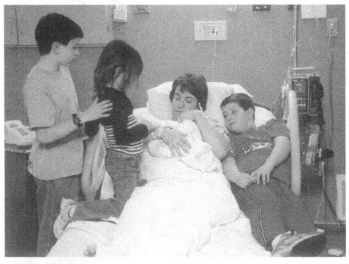

Kids seeing Grace on hospital bed with me holding Grace

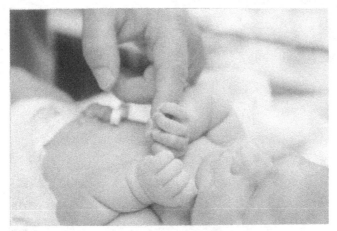

Grace holding Rich's finger

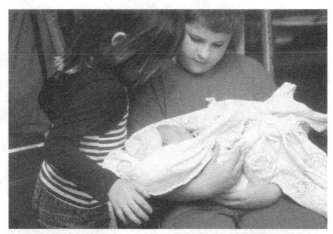

3

It's All About Perspective

The kids were elated to have Grace home. We all were, but they were ready to be Mommy's helpers in taking care of all the baby needs. They still had some fear in their eyes, but mostly joy each time they saw Grace and held her. With the arrival of a new baby at our home came the normal new adjustments to life, but this baby came with many more as well. The grandmothers had both stayed to help out with the children and Grace. While I appreciated their help, I knew that they just wanted more time with Grace. We all still had in the back of our minds the death sentence that the doctors had given her. There was no way to rid ourselves of that thought.

Our house was very quickly overwhelmed by the hospice team. They were there to be helpful and supportive to our family. Some members of the team would come to help us make "memory" items such as hand molds. These were wonderful ideas, but I knew what they were truly for. They were for the day that Grace would no longer be with us. The chaplain came to give spiritual support but didn't come much after he realized we already had a good church family and a pastor who met that need for us. Two wonderful nurses came daily to check on Grace's condition, check her weight, and how she was nursing. They were very caring and quickly fell in love with our Grace. They were a constant daily reminder that our time with Grace was going to be short, according to them. They were there to keep up with her progress in her decline and help us through it.

When Grace was born in the afternoon of Tuesday, April 10, she weighed 6 lbs. 11.9 oz! That was more than my firstborn had weighed! Eric weighed in at 6 lbs. 11.5 oz. By late afternoon on Thursday, April 12, when we were discharged to go home, she weighed 6 lbs. 2.7 oz. On Friday when the hospice nurses came in the afternoon, Grace had dropped to 5 lbs. 15 oz. I was thinking that she was not nursing the best, but she was still nursing. She was such a good baby because she was sleeping a lot. I had to wake her up to nurse her. When the nurse checked her over, she just kept saying over and over how Grace was so weak and that was why she was only sleeping and wouldn't wake up to eat. As she kept saying "weak," I felt like my crowded house was closing in on me. She took blood to check Grace's bilirubin level. This was to help her know if Grace was jaundiced. Little did I know that this would be the first of many needles and pokes through Grace's life. Grace was jaundiced and would need to be treated for that, but thankfully that could be done at home. The nurse would come daily to do a blood draw from Grace until her levels were good and the jaundice was gone. As the nurse spoke about how weak Grace was, she said that we needed to start a bottle to supplement her since my milk was not in yet and it was too hard for Grace to get enough. She wanted us to be able to measure how much Grace was eating. She said the next step would be to put a feeding tube in Grace if the bottle did not work. I just kept thinking that surely God did not bring Grace home just to die in the next few days. Some family had come by then, and my mother-in-law could tell I was getting upset and anxious during that nurse's visit. She was very gracious to help keep people out of the living room. It was our first full day at home and many friends and church family kept coming to the door to drop off gifts, food, visit, and see this special girl.

As the nurse left, we knew we had to get this bottle plan into action. My mother-in-law and sister-in-law went to the store to buy a pump. I wanted to do the absolute best for Gracie to make her healthy, so I would be pumping very soon. We dug out all the bottles in our home. There were not too many considering I had nursed all of my other children. We quickly started attempting to feed Grace by bottle. I would hold her and put the nipple in her mouth and she looked like she was eating, but when I tipped the bottle back around to check her progress, nothing had been eaten! This went on for every bottle I had! I soon realized that Grace had the appearance of eating when I nursed her but did not have the strength to actually get any milk. With each bottle I tried, I was feeling more and more panicked, worried, and scared. The kids were being kept busy with their cousins who had come to town, but I know the grandmothers and aunts who were now present could feel and share in my concern. This precious child could not get stronger if she could not get any nourishment. The nurse would be back the next day but Grace's weight would continue to drop. We had to get her fed.

Right about the time my fear was escalating after trying three different bottles with none of them working for Grace, more family arrived. It was Rich's brother and his family from Minneapolis. They came in very excited and joyful to see our miracle baby, but quickly could tell that something was terribly wrong. I told them that we were not getting any food into Grace and she was losing weight and strength. My sister-in-law, Mary, calmly came over to where I was holding Grace on the couch. She put her finger in Grace's mouth and knew from her speech therapy job exactly what kind of bottle Grace needed. She promptly got on the phone trying to find the Haberman bottle. Finally, at 11:00 p.m., Mary and Lisa, my sweet sisters-in-law, went to Bergan Mercy Hospital and brought back a similar bottle called a Pigeon that is often used for babies with cleft-palate lips. When they arrived back at home, Grace immediately drank from this bottle and we all knew that it was God's hand that had taken care of our fears and our sweet Grace. I had no idea that a speech therapist also worked with feeding and eating issues. Mary's strong and calm presence as well as her expertise in her field were exactly what we needed, and God had brought her clear from Minnesota to give us her special knowledge at exactly the moment Grace needed it! On Saturday, when the hospice nurse came back to our home, Grace weighed in at 6 lbs.; how thrilled we all were that we were finally headed in the right direction.

The bilirubin lights, used to treat newborn jaundice, arrived on Friday, which also was very overwhelming. They had just showed up at the door with no one actually calling to tell me they were coming. The light treatments were a dual blessing because it made the nurses come out daily for five days to check Grace's blood to make sure her jaundice was getting better, and we also got daily weight checks and knew that she was continuing to grow. By Sunday she was 6 lbs. 2.5 oz.; by Monday she'd only gained three-and-a-half ounces and was 6 lbs. 6 oz.; and Tuesday she weighed 6 lbs. 8.8 oz., gaining just under three ounces.

Our kids went to a Christian school that had been praying and praying for our little baby to live. All the teachers and staff knew of our situation and the children in each of my children's classrooms were praying. My friend Robin was a teacher there. She told me that the day after Grace was born was like a big happy party at school! Everyone knew that our incredible God had done this amazing miracle. The kids went back to school that week. I knew they needed to get back into their normal routine even though I could tell that they were fearful of what may happen to Grace while they were gone.

My sister-in-law stayed for a week and a half to help, my mother-in-law had to get back to teaching school, and my mother stayed for a while. I do believe my mom would have stayed for as long as I would let her. She was very helpful and good with Grace and the kids, but after a time, I needed to send her home. I felt like we were on the death watch, just watching and waiting. I could not live like that anymore. I could not get back to normal life until it was just our family.

It was interesting watching Megan through the next few weeks. She asked me daily about the Trisomy 13 and the Dandy-Walker brain malformations. She was only five years old and trying so hard to process this all. She asked, "Why did God have to give that to Grace?" For the first time in those weeks she cried about the possibility of Grace dying. One day she came home from preschool saying that her teacher did not know what Tri 13 was. That was Megan's way of saying Trisomy.

***

After Grace got off the lights for her jaundice, we had the go-ahead to leave the house. So we did! Grace went to ball games, parent lunches, concerts at school, Track and Field day, even a field trip to the park. Everyone was so thrilled to see her! I remember our very first time back in church as a family. Grace was in my arms. How wonderful it was! Our worship team led everyone in singing "How Can I Keep From Singing" by Chris Tomlin.

This song felt like a gift from God. It told of the victory in Christ, just like the one that our family had just experienced. I knew from singing that song that God had already done exceedingly and abundantly more than I had asked! I felt like I had no right to expect more or even to ask for more, but it was my responsibility now just to praise Him for all He had done. What an emotional and victorious day that was!

We were so very blessed for the gal from the organization "Now I Lay Me Down to Sleep" to come back to our home and take pictures once again, this time of our whole family alive and well! The pictures she took will forever be treasured. The weeks after that day at church were filled with ups and downs, but mostly ups. It was incredible to realize each day that God chose our family in which to place this beautiful miracle. Of course Grace had come with the normal newborn challenges like lack of sleep, but with her these challenges were more difficult than normal. She really had her days and nights mixed up. She still had not opened her eyes so without the visual light and dark it was very tricky. We worked hard to keep her awake during the day in hopes of sleep at night but to no avail. Before she was born, we had bought new furniture for our empty living room. We had only bought a loveseat and a chair because we already had a piano in the room and didn't feel the need for the couch at that time. It would crowd things up! Since Grace wasn't sleeping, I made that loveseat my sleeping place for the next couple months and kept her bassinet right next to it. That way I could see and hear her every breath while she was sleeping at night as well as during the day. Needless to say, between the short loveseat and Grace's lack of sleeping, I did not get much sleep through those months. Grace's feeding process was also very time consuming. I would nurse her, then feed her a bottle, and then pump for the next feeding. This also had to be done around the clock to make sure she was eating enough.

The tough, difficult moments came mostly when the nurse would come for her visit. She thought it was important for me to stay in the reality. She would tell me daily that even though Grace appeared to be doing well, *she was not here to stay.* She thought it was so important that I remember that. She also thought it was important that we have oxygen at our house so we would have it for when we needed it. I wasn't sure when that time would be, but I trusted her and thought it was better to be safe, so it was ordered.

The day the oxygen came was a very hard day. I had to learn how to use it and then they wanted me to practice using it. It just seemed like a very difficult thing to learn and do at that time when I was already so busy and exhausted. We did work at it every once in a while. Grace did get very purple when she got upset, and the nurses thought her oxygen levels were getting low. Some days I was just so tired that I was extra emotional. Rich kept reminding me of a quote I had shared with him during the pregnancy. I had read it in a wonderful book given to me by a friend, *Holding on to Hope* by Nancy Guthrie, "Worry does not rid us of tomorrow's sorrow; it just robs us of today's joy."

He was so right, and it did me such good for him to remind me. It just seemed so much easier to worry because I felt totally responsible for Grace. I felt responsible for whether she ate and how much she ate, if she grew, if she conserved her energy so she didn't burn too many calories, making sure her reflux did not get down in her lungs, and calming her quickly so that her oxygen levels did not go too low for too long. I knew that God was ultimately in control and that nothing I did or did not do would change Grace's fate, but it sure was hard to not feel like I could help control that.

On April 30, 2007, my journal read: "She is so precious, Lord. I just really desire for her life to be long."

Our perinatologist had told us that these four things could take Grace's life in the months to come:

1. Failure to thrive – she stops eating and growing.

2. Apneic episode – she stops breathing in her sleep.

3. Reflux getting in her lungs and causing pneumonia.

4. Dandy-Walker brain malformation – the fluid on the brain.

Sometimes knowing these things just made life harder. How does a person not live in fear? How do you not have these things at the front of your mind and not feel like you are responsible to keep them from happening? I had been an elementary school teacher; I'd never been in the health field. Would I even know how to tell if one of these things were happening? I was learning more each day, but it was overwhelming. I did not know of anyone who had walked down this path before. There was really no one I could talk to who understood or had answers to my many questions.

Grace's body temperature had always been lower than normal, so the hospice nurses had me dressing her with an extra layer of clothing. This way she would not need to burn extra calories by trying to keep her body temperature up. Later in April, I noticed that Grace was too warm. I thought it was because I had too many clothes on her. Then that night she was so hot I realized that she had a fever. She was sleeping a lot and not eating again. It was hard for me not to be angry with the child who had passed the fever on to her. None of my other kids got the illness. Grace lost weight again, which immediately put fear in me. Then I was reminded of Joseph in the Bible. Although his brothers had sold him into slavery, God had used it for good. I took Grace to her pediatrician on Monday. She suggested cutting the nipples in the bottle more and adding calories by putting formula into the breast milk. Grace gained 6 oz. in two days! It was amazing. I was starting to see how God orchestrates every little detail in our lives, and in Grace's life, to accomplish His purposes. Without the sick child, there was no fever. Without the fever, no doctor's visit. Without the doctor's visit, no new insight for Grace to be able to gain more calories and weight. I praised God for His great wisdom and even for the sick child!

In May we celebrated Mother's Day as well as Grace's one month birthday! What a special day! I had envisioned just months earlier that I would not even want to celebrate Mother's Day, expecting to have lost a baby, and here we were with four beautiful children.

On May 30, 2007, our two nurses came again for our weekly checkup. Grace weighed in at 8 lbs. 4 oz. A perfect weight gain in my eyes! I couldn't believe it when they started talking about making sure she didn't gain too much weight each day because that could make it difficult for her to breathe. How did we manage to go so quickly from one concern to another? Both nurses were quite happy with how well Grace was doing. Grace's head measured 36 cm, which is an appropriate growth amount since birth. Nothing too visible appeared from her Dandy-Walker brain malformation yet. They also talked about having one of them stop coming for the checkups so as to save our insured hospice days for later when Grace may really need it. I started wondering, *At what point do we just get to live like she is not going to die?* Would that day ever come?

At the end of their visit I asked if they would like to see Grace's birth video. They both wanted to watch it and loved it. The gal from "Now I Lay Me Down to Sleep" had done a wonderful job. The nurse who would be leaving us soon I was sure had a relationship with Jesus, but the other nurse I was unsure of. She was quite teary eyed during the video. Later she told me of another family whose Trisomy 13 baby had lived for five months but had many issues that Grace did not have. The nurse told me how she and our pediatrician had been talking and they were both amazed that Grace was not on a feeding tube yet. They were feeling quite optimistic about Grace, and yet she always added, "I don't want to get your hopes up. We still need to be realistic." Then she talked about how she believed there was a reason for everything and we just needed to look for it. She left and came back in with a Christmas dress that had belonged to her granddaughter and was sized for a nine-month-old. She wanted to give it to Grace. A Christmas dress in May! Maybe she had more hope that Grace was going to live longer than even she expected! I am not sure how the conversation turned, but as she walked out the door she said, "He sure was listening to your prayers." I knew that God had many reasons for all of this and I am thankful that He has shown us some. I truly believed that one of them was for our nurses and hospice team to see Jesus. God was already allowing that to happen!

May was a very busy month with baseball games and other end-of-the-school-year activities. Grace handled most things well, especially if I timed her feedings correctly or had a bottle available. She loved being outside. I took her to the boys' classrooms before school got out. Ethan was very proud to have her in his classroom. His teacher and some students prayed for her. This class had been perfect for Ethan this year. I remember one day at parent lunch one of the moms told me she had been in the classroom and Ethan had teared up. So at his lunchtime I checked on him. I knew he had a substitute teacher that day. When I asked him what had happened, he said that she had asked about their families and he had shared about Grace. Then he looked at me with big eyes and said, "Mom, about seventeen of the kids in class prayed for Grace and our family!" I could tell how much that meant to him. I know I was very preoccupied with Grace during this time, so it was so good to see that God was growing the faith in my children too. He was surrounding them with who they needed, to encourage them, to give them hope. What a loving God He is.

The month of June flew by. We celebrated Grace's two-month birthday at the Widman farm in Iowa! Many people, both family and friends who had not been able to meet Grace made a special trip to the farm to see her. She met great grandparents, aunts and uncles, great aunts and great uncles, cousins, and many more members of our extended families. She was held and loved on by many. She drank well from her bottle and was very happy. Once we were back in Omaha she went on outings to the park, to so many baseball games that her car seat smelled like the ballfield, and she also went on her first run with Mommy in the jogging stroller. She didn't seem to mind the bumps and slept through it all. When we were home she received many visitors from church and family as well. God was so good to bring many others alongside us for this journey. It was an overall good month with Grace eating about three ounces a feeding and burping. The toughest part was the nights. She was still very mixed up with her days and nights. She would wake up every one or two hours so I was still totally exhausted. She was definitely worth every tiring, difficult, and worrisome moment. Her sweet little smile was so precious. Each of the kids loved her so much and had their own special way of calming her and loving her.

July proved to be a much more difficult month. Besides the lack of sleep for the first part of the month, Grace had started to reflux (choke). She also had an ear infection. So she decided to stop eating most of the time. She made gurgling sounds and just wouldn't swallow. Her feedings became 2/3 of an ounce or one ounce at the most. Many feedings she wouldn't want any. We took her in to the doctor and she put Grace on Prevacid for the reflux and amoxicillin for the ear infection. Three nights later I took Grace to Bergan's Pediatrics Express. I prayed for an understanding doctor who would not dismiss my Trisomy 13 baby as not worth treating. God answered. My pediatrician's partner was working and she was familiar with Grace already. After hearing how little Grace was eating, she started her on Pedialyte every hour for twenty-four hours. She said to keep using the Prevacid, but also to use Mylanta. I took Grace home and she really liked the cherry flavored Mylanta. It seemed to be working. Grace was not in nearly as much pain so she would eat, just not big amounts. I took Grace back to the pediatrician a few days later. As she looked at the overall picture, she showed me on the infant weight chart that Grace had gone from the tenth percentile last month to the fourth percentile this month. She thought we needed to be admitted to the hospital for a feeding tube. I was not ready for this and talked her into waiting until the next Monday, thinking, *Surely Grace will pick up on her feedings.*

***

Unfortunately Grace did not eat much over the weekend. She went long timeframes without eating at all. She would not eat from 10:00 p.m. to 6:00 a.m. and then again from 11:00 a.m. to 7:00 p.m. By Monday I was ready for the feeding tube. Our pediatrician had said that Grace needed to gain two ounces by Monday and she had only gained one. I could not stand by and watch her starve to death. I had our bags packed and we were aiming to stay with Grace at the hospital. We were admitted by 11:00 a.m. on July 16. She had a NG (nasogastric) tube put in. This is a thin feeding tube that is placed through the nose into the stomach. They started the tube feedings right away.

Getting the tube in was quite difficult. It took two tries and two x-rays. I had thought they were going to teach me how to do it all but they did not. They just monitored Grace to make sure she was handling it well. She did, so we were discharged on Tuesday at 5:00 p.m. That night a nurse came out to show me how to run the feeding pump. I had to listen to Grace's stomach with a stethoscope as I pushed air through a syringe into the feeding tube in her nose. This was to check and make sure that the tube was still in her stomach. I was very nervous about having the air go in. I didn't feel like I knew what it sounded like. On the first try I pushed too much and poor Grace had too much air in her tummy. She threw it up and choked soon after she was done. Then at bedtime I prayed, "Lord, help the tube to be in the right spot because you know I am very unsure." The feeding seemed to go well through that night. Then in the morning I listened to her tummy for a long time. That time I could tell what I was listening for. By Wednesday morning Grace had thrown up her feed again and began choking and gagging more frequently. The rest of the feedings went well, but I had to watch Grace so carefully for when she gagged. She could hardly work it out on her own. I was thankful that my mother-in-law had taken the kids back to the farm with her. Wednesday afternoon's feeding went well. I thought I was finally starting to get it down. I got her to bed that night at 10:30 and we were having our first great night's sleep since she had been on the all-night feeds. Then at 5:00 am I woke up to hear Grace choking. I got her out of bed, held her upright, and patted her back to help her through it. I spent the next two hours crying. I was so afraid. Afraid that I would make a mistake. Afraid that she would aspirate, get pneumonia, and die.

On that Thursday, Grace wasn't breathing well in the morning, but seemed to get better through the day. She was choking and gagging a lot that day and I was crying a lot. I had gone from weeks of optimism, thinking that she might live to her first birthday, back to the thought that we were going to lose her any time. I told Rich that I thought we needed an apnea monitor. It would tell us when she was choking and gagging. I thought that I would be okay if God had her stop breathing in her sleep, but I didn't think I could handle it if she choked and gagged and I wasn't there for her. So that day we got the apnea monitor and a suction machine. I learned how to use them both. That night it took us a while to get Grace to bed with the monitor and the feeding pump. We were in bed by 11:00 and she slept until 7:00 the next morning. The monitor went off at 3:00 a.m., but Grace was fine. I slept much better.

Then Friday came with more breathing problems. It started like it had on Thursday, but it did not progressively get better through the day. I spent a lot of time on the phone with the nurses from the hospital as well as hospice. They kept trying to figure out the cause. I had Grace on oxygen all day, but as I watched her body move with each breath and her little chest go in and out, I knew it was not good. At about 4:00 p.m. I had the nurse listen to her over the phone, and it was then that she said, "You need to get her in." Fortunately, my pediatrician's partner waited for me to get Grace to the office before she left for the day. The doctor's office was on the west side of the hospital. She checked Grace's oxygen level and it was in the 60s. A normal pulse oxygen level should be in the high 90s, so Grace was in danger. Grace was very blue by this time. The doctor and I literally ran Grace from the west side of the hospital full of offices to the east side of the hospital to a room that was waiting for her. It seemed like such a long run with Grace in my arms in distress. The whole way running over there the doctor kept asking me, "Now you're sure you want to do this? I just want to make sure we are on the same page. You want to do everything, right?"

My regular pediatrician and I had just had our "DNR" talk on the previous Monday when we were admitted for the feeding tube. Since Grace was born, we had a "Do Not Resuscitate" order from the doctor. This was simply stating that we would not go to extraordinary measures to save her life. To be honest, when we got that order, I had no idea how many aspects there really were to be considered. I didn't even realize that the differences in the anomalies in the lives of these Trisomy kids could be so vast. Some kids had many obvious problems at birth, seen or unseen, and some kids did not have many problems at all. Some problems had to be dealt with right away, and others may not need to be dealt with for quite some time or even at all. It had been explained to me that one of the main reasons for having a DNR order was so that if you came upon your child and found that your child had passed away, when the paramedics or firefighters came, they would not give CPR and try to resuscitate your child. Without the DNR, they would be required by law to try to resuscitate her. The doctor also explained that just because you had the DNR did not mean that you had to abide by it no matter what. You could rescind it at any time or simply not show it. When I talked with the doctor on Monday, I told her we still wanted it. She could tell I didn't really, but I was able to tell her, "My God is bigger than a DNR." That I really did believe. Now, just three days later, I was on my way to the hospital with Grace in a critical state. I had called Rich on the way to ask him about the DNR and make sure we were on the same page. We wanted to stabilize her to see what was wrong by whatever means was necessary, then we could decide what needed to be done.

When we reached the room they had ready for Grace, we were surrounded by nurses. There were at least ten to twelve nurses working on Grace. I was very scared and unsure of what was even happening, so I called Rich to have him come right away. Thankfully he worked close by. They took Grace's vitals and intubated her right away. It was absolutely awful to watch. I had never seen anything like that before. They couldn't get the tube down her in the first two tries. They tried four times to get an IV started in the vein in her little foot. I was so thankful when Rich got there. I had called many people for prayer and I know my parents got in the car right away to come. Rich's mom, along with Lisa and the kids, had made it back to Omaha. They made many calls asking for prayer.

A chaplain from the hospital came to be with us. It was then that I realized the severity of the situation. They talked about getting Grace over to the children's hospital by ambulance. Before we even left, they had x-rays done on her and had determined that she had pneumonia. They also ran many other blood tests. There was a moment in all of this that the doctor and I were standing side by side, looking at Grace all hooked up to the monitors. She said to me, "I think she is just very tired." Somehow I felt like she was implying that Grace was tired of living but I didn't want to believe it. So I confirmed it with her by asking, "You mean of living?" She answered, "Yes." She may not have meant to, but she made me feel like I was making sweet little Grace suffer and go through all of this just for me. I didn't realize it at the time, but this was a question that I would ask myself many times during the weeks and months to come, *Why does this sweet child have to suffer?*

I rode in the ambulance with Grace. The driver happened to be a Christian dad of a sweet girl I had coached in volleyball at the Christian school where I worked. I appreciated how God kept bringing familiar people into our storm. He gave us a glimmer of light and hope in knowing that He was with us, He was in control, and we could trust His plan.

When we got to the children's hospital, we were taken straight to our room in the PICU (Pediatric Intensive Care Unit), never expecting we would be there so long. We were blessed with many visitors, both friends and family. We definitely were not alone. Our church body, friends, and family helped take care of our every need as I stayed with Grace in the hospital and Rich managed the three kids at home.

The next morning the doctor from the other hospital came to do her rounds at this hospital. This time she told me that she was talking more as "a friend." I wish she hadn't said that. She said, "I really think Grace was trying to go yesterday." I was trying to understand what she was telling me and trying to make her understand my thoughts. I told her that we really didn't want Grace to suffer and she responded with, "Well, she is suffering. Look at her, with all the tubes and the needles." She told me that she thought this situation—Grace aspirating, getting pneumonia from it, and being in the hospital—would continue happening. She said that eventually parents are just ready to let babies like Grace go. Then she said, "But I understand, you have to be okay with it." That was so incredibly hard to hear. I could not think that I would ever truly be "ready" or "okay" with letting her go.

July 21, 2007, from my journal: "I just pray that God will give Rich and I wisdom to know what to do and that He will give us the strength that we need, if and when that time will come. I also pray that God will take her in His perfect timing, and that it will never be a decision that we have to make."

That hospital stay was very difficult. It would be the first of many and I didn't realize at the time that the things I did there would become routine for Grace and for me. Each night before bed I would sit or stand by Grace's bedside touching her. I would sing to her and read Scripture and pray with her. I told her each night that if Jesus wanted to take her home to heaven, she should go, that it was okay. We would not be separated for very long.

Most of the doctors and nurses were very good and caring, but with some doctors, you could just see it in their eyes—the look of "Why are you going to all this trouble for this child?" One doctor seemed especially cold and callous and of course we had her for three of our days there. I had been listening to the local Christian radio station there, and Monday night they were taking requests. I needed some encouragement so I picked up the phone not really expecting anyone to answer. Instead it was answered on the first ring! I briefly told the woman who answered our story of Grace being in the hospital with pneumonia and requested our song of hope and victory, Chris Tomlin's "How Can I Keep From Singing." She said that she would play it within the hour. So I took Grace in my arms and held her for that entire hour. Finally, at the end of the hour came my song. As the song started playing I realized that she must have forgotten which song I had requested, but God knew. She played Casting Crowns' "Praise You In This Storm," our forever personal song given by God for this time in our life. I sat in that chair holding Grace while the tears ran down my face, thanking God once again for showing me so incredibly that He was with us through all of this. We could trust Him and lean on Him.

At the end of the song, our very unfriendly PICU doctor came into our room. There was no hiding my tears. She didn't ask, but I told her what had just happened. I explained the significance of the songs and how God had just reminded me that He was with us and in control of everything. She did not say anything, but I was thankful God had given me the opportunity and courage to be bold in declaring my faith. By the end of our stay, when that doctor saw me in the cafeteria, she asked how things were going. I told her things were good and we would be going home soon. She said, "I hope it goes well for you." This was the most kind and sincere response that I had ever received from her and certainly it was unexpected. God is always working.

That stay continued to be tough. I think much of it was difficult for me because I was quite new to the medical world, and now I was getting a BIG dose of it on my precious little baby girl. In the end, though, God was very good to take care of Grace. He helped her get the help she needed to save her life, and then allowed her to come off the respirator with no problems. The tests that were done helped us to see the need for a nasojejunal (NJ) feeding tube, and that was put in while we were there. This still went through her nose but went farther into her intestines so she was less likely to aspirate the food. The best part of the stay was on a Sunday night when Grace's tummy was finally full and the respirator was gone and Grace cooed and babbled to me for a half hour! Then Monday and Tuesday mornings I woke up to her sweet cooing. One morning she babbled to me for one and a half hours! It was so amazing and sweet that God could bless us this way. His tender reassurances told me that it was all worth it. On Tuesday and Wednesday I made a big effort to have someone come stay with Grace so I could go home and spend time with Eric, Ethan, and Megan. They had been able to go to the farm and spend lots of time with grandparents and cousins. They were all very glad to see me and I said, "You guys have been having so much fun!" Ethan looked me in the eyes and said, "Yes, but we've had enough." Even Megan was ready to send her Grandmas home. What a shock!

Being released from the hospital was so sweet, but also a bit stressful. We had difficulty getting the medicines we needed and then Grace fussed all that night. At about 3:30 a.m. I realized that Grace had pulled her NJ tube out at least an inch and a half. In a panic, I shoved it back in. Then I spent the rest of the night crying and praying to God that I hadn't hurt her and listening to see if she would reflux and aspirate again. This was all so new to me that shutting her feeds off never crossed my mind. It was an awful night. The next day we went in for an x-ray and thankfully the tube was still in the right place.

August was a much better month. Grace was steadily gaining weight. Who wouldn't? She was eating twenty-four hours a day! I was getting much more comfortable in my role as nurse. I kept all of her medications written down with their times and checked them off as I did them. One weekend Rich went out of town and I decided it was time for me and Grace to get back in the bedroom. Four months of sleeping on the living room loveseat with not much sleep was really starting to wear on me. So I put the crib up in the bedroom and every time Grace slept for naps or at nighttime, that is where she was. Nights were still rough, but by the time Rich returned she was doing fairly well. Every night when I put Grace to bed I would stand and rock her back and forth as I did with all of my children and I would sing to her just as I had sung to them. Each child had their own songs that I would consistently sing each night. For Grace, I always sang, "I Love You, Lord," "I Cast All My Cares," "Lord, You Are More Precious," and "Jesus, Jesus, Jesus." These songs always seemed to calm her and me. They were my way of praising God and laying it all at His feet every night before I went to sleep. I do think that God blessed that, because regardless of how much sleep I was able to get or how many hours I was awake with Grace, when my head hit the pillow I slept peacefully. The worries of the day and the possible ones of the night were always gone.

***

Grace started talking and smiling more. She smiled in response to talking, tickling, and kissing. I put blankets on her in bed or when she was in her bouncy seat and she kicked them off! I know that for the normal child these do not necessarily make the big highlight reel, but for Grace, every little thing she did was big. By August, I was feeling like I was doing better emotionally most of the time. The first few months whenever I saw a baby anywhere, my first thought would be healthy baby. I am not sure if I was envious or if I was just staying in the reality that Grace was not healthy and I so wished that she could be. I also was having a difficult time when other moms tried comparing their baby to Grace. I would find myself thinking that they and their child were nothing like Grace and me. How could they even try to compare? Did they ever have the thought that I had every month, "What will I dress my baby in for her funeral?" Every month I had a dress or outfit that I had already picked out in my head. Maybe I was more fearful than I thought I was of what the future held. I didn't feel like Grace's death was ever-present in my thoughts. I think it was just the reality. At her birth I planned for reality and hoped for a miracle. Hopefully God would continue to perform daily miracles as he allowed her to stay with us.

The month of September went by quickly. We still had challenges with Grace spitting up, having too many secretions, trying to figure out the right balance of medications, trips to the ER to check the placement of her tube, and then discussing with the surgeon what our choices were for Grace to get a more permanent solution for her feeding tube and scheduling the surgery. The surgery would put a gastrojejunostomy (GJ) feeding tube in through her stomach wall that went right into her jejunum, bypassing her stomach and going into her intestines. The tube through her nose would not be needed anymore. Though Megan was sick for the ten days leading up to Grace's surgery, God totally protected Grace and kept her healthy for her surgery. Sometimes I thought my prayers to God must be so confusing to Him. As I prayed those weeks for Grace to be healthy for the surgery, as the days got closer to it, I prayed that He would make Grace be sick if she should not have the surgery. I think I just always had doubts as to whether we were doing what was best for her, always remembering that with every surgery or procedure came added risks to Grace's life. In my confusing way, I was just praying for God's will to be done, His good and perfect will. Even with all of that, the month seemed to be calmer.

The night before the surgery I took the older three kids to a friend's house and put them to bed. I could see the fear in sweet little Megan's eyes as she asked one more time about Grace's surgery. I reassured her that Grace would be fine and Jesus would be watching over her. This was all so tough for us adults to understand and deal with, I could not imagine how difficult it must have been for a six-year-old. All of my sweet kids loved Grace so much that it was a tough burden to carry. I just kept trying to show them that we needed to keep giving it all to God and that we could trust Him.

The morning of the surgery, Grace and I were at the hospital by 8:05 a.m. As I filled out the paperwork, I wondered why all the history and medical information on Grace had to be done again even when it was the same hospital we had spent so much time in just a couple months before. They checked Grace's vital signs and weighed her in at 12 lbs. and 9 oz. Grace had slept really well the two nights and the day before. I knew God was helping her and me get the rest we would need. One of our pastors and his wife came to pray with us at 8:30 a.m. We had a student nurse who had been coming out to the house weekly for several weeks. She had received permission to observe the surgery. Even though she was a student nurse and could not do anything in the operating room, it gave me comfort to know that she would be in there with Grace. She knew Grace and everyone who knew Grace, loved her. That was a blessing for me.

The anesthesiologist came in and started talking to me about Grace needing platelets because her labs were low. I said, "They didn't do any labs on her." Thankfully they realized then that they were looking at the wrong chart! A second person came in and started checking Grace over. He asked me, "Where is her trach? When did you have her trach taken out?" Again the wrong chart. Our student nurse looked at me and said with a smile, "Don't worry, I won't let them do anything to her except the GJ tube." That was reassuring to me. Then the surgeon came to see me and he thankfully knew exactly what he was doing. They wheeled Grace away at 10:10 a.m. I hadn't realized they were going to intubate her and that made me a bit more nervous. I was so thankful Rich was at the hospital with me through her surgery. It took longer than the doctor had said it would take, which also causes a momma's heart to worry. Thankfully when the doctor came out at noon, he said that Grace did well with the surgery and everything went as planned. Grace did well with her feedings in the hospital and we were able to take her home the next day.

Grace did really well for the first few days, but by Sunday she was starting to be more agitated. By the next Tuesday, on October 2, Grace's new tube site was infected. By Friday, Grace was leaking nasty green fluid out of her tube site and some blood as well. We were admitted back into the children's hospital that day. Grace had started throwing up formula that morning, so I knew her tube wasn't in the right place. We had known it had moved from the jejunum into the duodenum. I knew she should not have had formula in her stomach to throw up. They had given her some pain medication since she was obviously hurting. We had shut off Grace's feeds on Friday when she started throwing up and they had admitted her, but she needed to go back into surgery with the radiologist to get it fixed. The surgeon wanted to wait until the next Monday to do it, which would have prevented Grace from eating for the whole weekend. Thankfully with some pushing and much praying, one of the surgeons decided he would come in to do it on Saturday. God showed His power and presence again. When the surgeon came out to report, he said that the radiologist would not have been able to fix it. The balloon that holds the tube in place had slipped out and was between the stomach and the abdomen wall, causing lots of pressure and pain for our sweet little girl. It was building up a lot of gas in her stomach and causing the bleeding and the green drainage. He was able to fix it and we were even able to go home late that Saturday night! God was so good!

***

I was finally feeling like I could breathe again by Tuesday. The anxiety of having our baby in the hospital with things far from our control was very great. Then on that afternoon, Grace's GJ tube clogged. We had just been to the surgeon that morning and he said I could take her off the pain medication she had been on. I was trying to get Tylenol down the tube when it clogged. I had learned that Coke can help unclog a feeding tube, so I attempted that several times. Finally, at 9:00 p.m. that night I still hadn't been able to unclog it so I took her to the ER. I knew Grace was getting a temperature again. She was 101.5° at home and by the time we got to the ER she was 102.6°. They didn't even work on her tube. They did vital signs, x-rays, and took blood to do lab tests. This was becoming an all-too-familiar whirlwind.

The next thing they told me was that Grace had a high white cell blood count, twice as high as it should be, 28,000. She also had a high electrolyte count which can cause the heart and brain to shut down. The longer we stayed the more they found wrong. She had high sodium, potassium, and hemoglobin. It was time to be admitted again. Only this time the hospital was full. We finally got in a treatment room by 2:00 a.m. By the time the nurses left the room it was 3:00 a.m. and Grace was fussy until about 5:00 a.m. The chair they gave me to sleep in was not comfy at all. They kept changing Grace's IV bag to meet the needs of all the high counts. They realized she was very dehydrated and said that can happen when you run a fever. Wednesday and Thursday went by and they still couldn't figure out what was wrong or why she was leaking all that green stuff from her stomach into the bag. Thankfully a nurse and a doctor saw how incredibly weary I was and got us into a normal room by Wednesday afternoon.

I was very emotional and scared. Every time I brought Grace to the hospital I was fearful that I would not be able to bring her home again. With all the unknowns about her condition, and all the things that kept popping up out of the blue that they could not even figure out, I was just filled with fear. They checked for a urinary infection and a blood infection. Also on Wednesday, a friend came to visit and brought a red rose. It was in honor of Grace's six-month birthday! I had been so consumed with everything happening that I had not taken time to reflect on the fact that Grace had lived for six months. What a gift! This was not how I had hoped to celebrate. Hopefully we would be able to take her home once again and celebrate. On Thursday they did an ultrasound of Grace's abdomen showing the kidney area again. They were looking for signs of infection. This was very hard to sit through. It took my mind back to my last ultrasound which was when Grace was diagnosed. I was terribly fearful of what they might find. They had not looked at that part of Grace's body yet. Her fever continued to be 102° until Thursday when it finally dropped to 100.8°. It finally got back to normal on Friday. They had also tested for mono thinking that maybe Megan had mono a month ago. Friday they sent us home without knowing what the problem had been. I was glad to be taking Grace home once again but also fearful. At this point, I was thinking that it would be just a matter of days until we were back in the hospital.

We had a rather calm weekend and then by Monday the student nurse came and thought that the tube site looked infected again. We called the doctor and had Grace put on an antibiotic. The next day we had an appointment with that doctor and he thought things looked good. He was not worried about the amount or color of the drainage. On Wednesday I was blessed to have a friend come stay with Grace while I went on a field trip with Ethan. He really wanted me to go. I think he just wanted his mom back doing the normal things I had always done. The field trip was fun and relaxing. I always enjoy seeing my kids interact with their friends and it was also good talking to one of my best friends who happened to be his teacher that year! Even though I had a few hours to put my focus elsewhere, at the end of the day, I was still incredibly exhausted. Grace's pediatrician had put Grace on some Canola oil (through her feeding tube) with the breast-milk on Monday in hopes of her gaining some weight. Unfortunately, it had made her constipated, and she was so uncomfortable that our nights were sleepless once again. I was at a loss to know how or when to get things done at home and even just getting some rest for myself seemed impossible.

By Thursday evening, Grace's feeding tube was clogged again. I had to shut it off. It happened again when I tried to put Tylenol in. I waited a little while to deal with it because I had to go out and get some fresh Coke with which to try to unclog it. They had given me a couple more tips in the hospital: using a smaller syringe would give me more pressure, and it also might help to push the syringe back and forth. I tried those ideas and could hardly get any Coke in. I worked at it for a couple hours before I took Grace to the ER at the children's hospital once again. The resident doctor was very nice and was working really hard so we could just go home. She was flushing Grace's feeding tube with more Coke when we heard a *pop* sound. Immediately after that I noticed that the tube was coming out farther than it had been. I knew it wasn't right and told the doctor. She then did an x-ray to check the placement of the tube, said it was good, and sent us home. I knew in my heart that it wasn't good, but I followed the doctor's instructions and we went home anyway.

Grace did well in the night, but then in the morning when I gave her medicine through the tube she got fussy. Then in the middle of her getting fussy, her feeding tube was coming out, way out! Please remember that I had no medical training! I was learning all of this as needed. So trying to stay and act calm while feeling so panicked on the inside was not easy. The tube was thicker at the point of entry while on the inside it was almost threadlike, it was so thin. Pushing something back in after it has been out could lead to infection, but something coming completely out could cause the surgery site (hole) in Grace's stomach to close up. I was unsure what to do once again. So I pushed a little bit in, and then taped the rest down to her stomach. I put a bandage wrap around it and pulled her shirt down while sobbing. I was so thankful that Grace almost always stayed calm through these moments. I could not imagine how much more difficult it would be if she were upset and crying. Then I quickly put Grace in her car seat, knowing that her being buckled in tightly would keep it all in place. She wouldn't be able to move enough to wiggle it out. I had called a friend the night before and shared my fears about the tube. She had told me to call her if I needed her and she would come. So I called her to come. I called a neighbor whose kids went to school with my kids and she came too, as did my mom who promptly packed and started driving the hour and a half to our home. I knew surgery would be needed yet again, so I packed a few things and Grace and I headed to the doctor's office.

At his office, I could tell the doctor was also frustrated. He knew surgery was needed again. Of course, I had cried most of the way there. I didn't know if this was happening as a result of what I was doing or if it was just happening. I told the Lord on that drive that I didn't think I could keep handling all of this. This day had just been so incredibly hard. We were admitted to the hospital and Grace was prepped for surgery again. For the third time, Grace had a feeding tube put in. When it was over, the doctor showed me that the balloon had broken, just as I had thought when I heard it pop in the ER, and he had replaced the tube with a GJ tube that was a bit wider. He said he doesn't normally put them in babies as small as Grace but hoped it might help with all of her clogging issues. Grace came out of surgery well and we were home two days later.

That month was very hard, being in and out of the hospital four times. I was starting to think that was how life was going to stay, but thankfully God was ready to give us some relief! As I look back on it, I remember how God always shows Himself in the midst of our storm.

If her tube had not clogged the first time, we would not have realized that Grace was so dehydrated and that all of her counts were so far off. Who knows what affect the mono would have had on her without the IVs and hospitalization?

I also believe that God's good plan for the other clogging and the doctor breaking the balloon was that we were able to get a better, wider feeding tube that appeared to be a much better fit for Grace. I started counting the days and weeks that we were out of the hospital!

***

In this crazy month, Rich had also been given a job opportunity in San Antonio, Texas. He had been at two different hotels in Omaha for a total of seven years, which is a pretty long stay in the hotel business. By October 22, Rich and I had to give his boss an answer if we would accept or not. We had been talking and praying about a job in Houston for a few weeks, and when we decided to pursue it, the company said they needed him in San Antonio instead.

Way back in the summer, I had a friend's husband come over to the house to look at all our projects that needed to be done. He was a "fix everything" guy. I'd called him because while I was walking up the stairs of our multi-level home one day, God had given me the feeling that I needed to get the house ready to sell. I needed to get things in order. This was new for me. I had agreed to moves before to support Rich and because it was a fun adventure. With the way our life had been recently, I didn't need any fun adventures. I needed calm, peace, stability, friends, and family close by for support. A move to a state so far away just would not have made sense, except God had prepared my heart simply by telling me to get my house in order. As Rich and I talked about it, everything just seemed right. On that morning, Rich gave me the opportunity to once again say no to moving. My response was full of doubts—"Well, maybe we shouldn't"—and I sent him off to work. Soon after that I called him and said, "I think you should take the job. I've had nothing but peace in all these weeks thinking and praying about it. I think we need to go."

As I thought through the process of finding a new house, new school, new church, new doctors, and new hospitals, God reminded me over and over that those were all just "little details" to Him. If we followed His plan, He would take care of the details, all of them. I honestly thought people would think we were nuts, but I knew we needed to go. Thankfully God made them all very supportive as we shared our news. Leaving our huge support system would be incredibly hard, but God would provide a new one. I was sure of that. I did feel guilty that we were taking the kids and especially Grace away from everyone who loved them all so much. I honestly felt like Grace was not just our baby, but everyone's baby!

I felt very strongly that Grace was a big part of why we were going. I thought that someone in Texas needed to meet our miracle girl. My grandmother thought that maybe God would help Grace get better medical care there.

Since we missed Grace's six-month birthday party with her in the hospital, we celebrated her seven-month birthday with many friends and family. It was a wonderful time to thank everyone who had been so helpful all those months. Rich had to leave fairly quickly for San Antonio to start work, while I had the job of staying back, getting the house sold, and taking care of the kids. Eric and Megan were excited about the move, but not Ethan. He was my shy one at the time and did not want to leave his friends. We prayed for lots of good friends in school, church, and our neighborhood. I knew that God would take care of their fears and worries, and also take care of mine.

At seven months old, Grace's smiles were very big when we tickled her. We went in for an MRI on November 15, 2007. I had read an article in the *Daily Bread* about an infant with micro-ophthalmia. This family had gone through the process of getting their child prosthetic eyes. The article said that without eyes in the sockets, the face would not form correctly and that could lead to other issues. When I asked the pediatrician about it, she thought the MRI was the first step to take. We also thought it would be a good opportunity to see how the Dandy-Walker brain malformation was looking. Would it look the same or had it changed or progressed at all? Sitting in the hospital on the day of the MRI, I was feeling quite relaxed. I realized how stressed I had recently been. Maybe I was just starting to get used to this new medical world we found ourselves thrown into or maybe I was starting to see that God was truly in control. Nothing was going to happen to our precious girl that was out of His control and He loved her more than I ever could.

Just a few days before Thanksgiving we were scheduled to see Grace's pediatrician and would find out the results of the MRI. While I was not too nervous about what the results would be, I was anxious to know. We had not seen any abnormal growth in Grace's head that would lead us to believe that the fluid was increasing, but it was the unseen that I feared the most. Grace and I were led back to the room and waited for the doctor to come in. As she came in, she was reading the MRI report. She told me about the diagnosis of the eyes. With micro-ophthalmia, the eyes are smaller than normal and set back far into the sockets. Then she continued reading out loud this time and said, "The Dandy-Walker malformation is gone." I said, "Gone?" She said, "I need a minute to process this." After looking at it for a couple more seconds, she said in disbelief, "It says the brain is normal."

The joy that came from that simple little sentence, "It says the brain is normal," was inexpressible. I felt like crying I was so happy, but I held off for a while. The doctor said that she would call the radiologist to confirm and she tried to explain that maybe the diagnosis was wrong to begin with from the ultrasound. There had to be a logical explanation in her mind, but not in mine! I said softly, "I just really believe God did a miracle." I knew in my heart that He had. I remembered so specifically the day the perinatologist pointed out on the ultrasound where the cerebellum was split and showing where the fluid was in between the two hemispheres. It wasn't misdiagnosed.

It was there and now it was not! I knew that God had done another huge miracle for our family and I spread the news as quickly as I could! I called Rich immediately and he was so happy to hear it. We went to the farm for Thanksgiving and shared with all the friends and family there. Then, that Sunday when we were able to be back at our own church in Omaha, we were all given the opportunity to share our praises. So I stood up with Grace in my arms and tears in my eyes and said, "Just in case any of you had forgotten how huge our God really is, we found out this week with an MRI that the brain malformation Grace had before birth is gone. Her brain looked normal. God did a miracle!" Ever since before her birth, I knew that God wanted me to give Him praise and glory and that is what I tried my best to do. He had done so many amazing things for us. How could I not?

***

I was thirty-eight years old when I gave birth to Grace. Just three years before, at age thirty-five, we were living in Omaha. Rich was doing his hotel job and I was doing what I loved, being a wife and mom. In our normal everyday activities something got in my eye. I thought that I had gotten it all out, but it was still bothering me so I made a doctor's appointment for myself. I had always had 20/20 vision and I just wanted to make sure that it was all out and that my eye had not been scratched. My physician, knowing that this was not his field of expertise, recommended that I see an ophthalmologist. The appointment was scheduled and off I went. The doctor had managed to get it all out of my eye and there was no scratch or damage done to my eye as a result. However, while the ophthalmologist was looking at my eye, he did a thorough exam and found something else. That was the day I found out that I had Fuchs' corneal dystrophy. I had never heard of it. He asked if there was any history of blindness in my family. There was none that I could recall. He went on to explain that this genetic disease is a slowly progressing corneal disease that was in both of my eyes. My eyes had guttata on the surface of my corneas that prevent my eyes from drying fluid off of them. These guttata would cause my vision to become cloudy due to the moisture that stays on my eyes. He told me that it eventually would lead to blindness unless we chose to do a corneal transplant at some point.

After having perfect vision my whole life, this diagnosis was totally unexpected. It immediately concerned me and brought fear into my mind and heart. The ophthalmologist gave me some drops for my eyes and sent me home to process this news. He had not given me a specific timeline. He simply had told me that it was a slow progressing disease. So I had time but no idea how much time. I went home in tears, fearful of what the future would hold for me. I cried for a few days as I researched it more. I joined a support group online. They were surprised I had been diagnosed that young. Most people do not get diagnosed until they are in their fifties or sixties. *Did that mean that my disease would progress faster? Would a transplant even be available some day when I am in need or would I be left to walk in darkness?* I tried to get answers to many questions, but in the end I just had to remember who knew all the answers. God did. In the next few years, the questions and the fears of having that disease would sit in the back of my mind. I knew I needed to just trust God with it completely, but it was much easier said than done. So there it sat.

Now, three years later, I was taking my baby to a pediatric ophthalmologist. Grace had not opened her eyes since the day she was born. This time the doctor was a friend I knew and trusted. Our boys went to the same school and played on the same baseball and basketball teams. He had known of our little miracle girl since before she was born. Even with all of this, I was fearful. He was going to open her little eyes. She had never opened them and I had never opened them. At the time I thought they may even be fused shut or that it would hurt her. Our goal was to find out if there was any possibility for sight. If she had any sight at all, it would disappear completely once we started putting prosthetic eyes in her sockets. If she had some sight, we did not want to take that away. My fear was not that she would not be able to see, but that it would be painful for her to have her eyes opened. Many times in those several months as Grace was introduced to people and I would explain to them what Trisomy 13 was, I would get the same comment about her not being able to see. "Oh, that's too bad that she cannot see." They felt so bad that she was blind! This just seemed ridiculous to me. Did they not hear me? She was not supposed to be alive! This was a very minor detail. My response to them every time was, "It's okay if she cannot see. We are just so thankful that she is alive!" They didn't seem to understand how happy we were that this baby we so desperately wanted was alive! The blindness, the feeding tube, and the other issues yet to be found were nothing in comparison to not having her with us at all! It was all in the perspective of how you looked at her. She was a precious life who was to be treasured and thankful for. She was a gift! We were so blessed just to have her with us.

Now, as I sought to get perspective on the way to this appointment, I was praying in the van and I kept asking God to give me a verse. Never doubt that God will give you what you need when you ask for it, because He does, and He did that day. The verse that God gave me was a verse I had learned in my years of working with the Cubbies (three- to five-year-old's) in our AWANA program at church. It is a wonderful program for kids to learn about Jesus and also to learn Scripture. Now, you can imagine that a verse that three- to five-year-olds are to learn is not huge and profound, but it was to me on that day. "Mine eyes have seen Thy salvation" from Luke 2:30. These words were spoken by Simeon when he saw the baby Jesus for the first time. This verse gave me so much comfort and peace that I was able to tell the Lord that I would rather He help Grace to see that Jesus loves her, more than I desired for her to be able to physically see. I prayed that God would help her to know Him and see Him in a special way.

While I had a peace that day at the appointment, I was not ready to look into her eyes. I had asked a friend to meet me there since Rich was in San Antonio. I was so grateful that she could look into Grace's eyes as well and confirm the news that the doctor had given me. While there were eyes, they were not formed correctly and he reassured me that there was no possibility for sight. I had always had a peace about Grace's blindness. Sometimes my mind wondered how we would overcome challenges and help her to learn, but I knew in my heart that God would give us what we needed when that time came. I praise the Lord for the perspective He gives and the reassurances He provides when we need reassurance most. I also praise Him for changing my perspective on my own diagnosis with my eyes. The fears of the future were suddenly just that, in the future. God was showing His day-by-day provision for everything that came our way with Grace. When the time comes that my eyesight becomes worse, I know that my trust will be in my God who will either provide ways to bring healing or He will help me through whatever dark days come.

***

December started out to be a very sweet month, except for the fact that Rich was gone working in San Antonio now. He would fly home for some weekends and we all looked forward to our time when he was there with us. With Grace's medical needs and the kids being in school, there was no way we could go spend time with him down in Texas yet.

By December Grace knew how to turn her head for a kiss! I would give her the cue, "kiss, kiss" and she would turn to us for her kiss! We all loved it and Grace gave and received many kisses from all of us each day. She had also learned to "kick." She had a wonderful piano toy that was meant to stimulate babies to kick and Grace loved to kick, which was no surprise to me considering how much she'd kicked in the womb!

Of course with Rich gone I had to rely on others for help with the occasional mishap. One day Megan locked Grace and my keys in the van. The house was locked and that key was also in the van. This was before the days that I had a cell phone. Yes, some panic set in with my special needs baby locked in the van. Thankfully she slept through it. I knocked on the door of our wonderful neighbors and they helped me call the realtor to come let me in the house where I would find another key. The police also came to help out with the crisis. I was so thankful for people who I could ask for help and I was actually getting much better at asking. The reality of my life now, whether Rich was home with me or not, was that I needed more help. I needed help with little things, like keeping my house clean and organized for showings so it would sell, and help with big things, like taking care of my older kids when a health crisis came up with Grace that sometimes needed quick action.

God had placed us in the perfect place with many caring friends, family, and even strangers to help us in our time of need. He had also given me a new song for the season. "Everlasting God" by Chris Tomlin came on the radio as I was desperately trying to clean the house and make it look just perfect for a showing. The words of the song were perfect, because I was so weary and I totally had to rely on strength coming from Him. Anyone who has sold a house knows that it is a lot of waiting . . . waiting for the first call from your realtor that your house will show, waiting while they look at your home, waiting for a call from your realtor, waiting to hear if they want a second showing, waiting to hear if they liked it, waiting to hear their pros and cons, and deciding if there is anything you can do to improve the cons, waiting for an offer.

I had to trust God would provide this strength for us, for me. He would provide it for every cleaning, before every showing, and in many more ways as we moved down to Texas. Surely, He would, wouldn't He?

On the evening of December 6, the older kids were all snug in their beds and I was enjoying my quiet time while holding Grace on the couch in the living room as we waited for Rich to fly in from San Antonio. I treasured these times with Grace, as I was not being pulled in every direction or having to balance getting everything else done with the kids, their schoolwork and activities, as well as keeping the house clean and in perfect condition for the possible showing. Since we had heard the Dandy-Walker brain malformation was gone, we were hoping that Grace would be spared seizure activity. I had always suspected Grace was having some seizure activity in a form called myoclonic jerks. She startled way too much. There was a substantial difference between her and my other babies, but every time I asked the many different doctors, I heard the same answer. The jerks would be rhythmic and almost able to be timed. This had never happened like that . . . until this night.

Grace had a few startles fairly close together and I knew it immediately. Her jerks had never been so many and so close together. I just continued to hold her, trying to comfort her. Then I just started sobbing and crying out to the Lord. I begged Him to stop them so that they would not hurt her or cause any damage to her brain. I also asked "Why?"—that question I thought a good Christian was not supposed to ask, but now as I have learned, is really okay to ask. How can you expect to get answers when you don't ask God the questions? So I asked. "Why does she have to have one more thing wrong with her? Why this now after we have just seen a miracle, when we are trying to prepare for a very big move? Why does she have to suffer? She is just an innocent precious little baby who has never done anything wrong or been mean to anyone!" Through the tears I started counting how many seconds in between her jerks and timing how long this seizure would last. I called the doctor's office and was told to take Grace to the ER. So I called a family friend to see if he could come be with the other kids at the house as they slept. He agreed and came quickly. I loaded Grace into the van and arrived at the ER at about 10:00 p.m. Of course, her seizure activity stopped on the ride there. She'd had the jerks every 15 to 45 seconds for 40 minutes straight. My poor baby. The people at the ER were very good. They took my report and observed her while checking her over. They gave her some medicine and sent us home with the advice to see a neurologist . . . another specialist. We got home quite late that night and thankfully, Rich got home shortly after. It was such a comfort knowing he was there with me, even if only for a short time. I was no longer alone, at least for the weekend.

On December 8, the neurologist was able to get Grace in for a visit. He was quite interested in Grace's history. He said, "If she had heart calcifications and now she doesn't, and if she had Dandy-Walker and now she doesn't, what makes you so sure she still has full Trisomy 13?" He also said, "Dandy-Walker doesn't just go away." He was implying that maybe the diagnosis was wrong. I told him that we had been shown on the ultrasound the two parts of her cerebellum split with the fluid in between. I also told him that I truly believed that God had done a miracle. He was a nice doctor, but of course, he had to remind me that Trisomy children don't live past five years of age. This was actually new news to me, better than the five minutes we had originally been told. He said that most of the children die early because of heart problems, but they die later because of brain problems. He also felt the need to have the DNR talk with me in a very extensive form. I didn't want to have that conversation the first time I had it with the pediatrician. I came to realize that it was apparently a necessary or required conversation that doctors had to have. I took it quite well in the office, staying strong and steady. It wasn't my first time hearing this information and I was sure it would not be my last, unfortunately.

Oh, how those words hurt later. I don't understand why doctors seem to have a need to be so negative and put such limits on these children's lives. I realize they have their statistics, but what are those really based on? Many people abort because they are given no hope and no information about the positive impact these kids have in our world, the love these kids have for others, and the joy that they are! For those who do not abort, many choose comfort care instead of taking normal medical steps that they would do in a heartbeat for a normal child. Again, this is frequently due to the advice given by doctors—doctors in whom we have placed our trust. After all, isn't it their job to heal the sick? Are they not highly trained and wise? Many doctors would advocate for comfort care because they do not think the quality of life that child might expect to live is worth living out. Unless a doctor truly knows a child with Trisomy 13, do they really know the quality of life that child has? Do they know how much they are loved? Do they see the smiles and hear the laughter? Only God really knows the potential of each child. Only God knows how many days that child will live, just as He is the only one who knows how long I will live. One of my favorite Scriptures I clung to was Psalm 139:13–16. I recited it while inserting both Grace and myself directly into the verse, making it personal.

> For You formed (Grace's) inward parts; You covered (Grace) in (my) womb. I will praise You, for (Grace) is fearfully and wonderfully made; Marvelous are Your works, And that my soul knows very well. (Grace's) frame was not hidden from You, When (Grace) was made in secret, And skillfully wrought in the lowest parts of the earth. Your eyes saw (Grace's) substance, being yet unformed. And in Your book they all were written, The days fashioned for (Grace), When as yet there were none of them. (Ps. 139:13–16, paraphrased)

I know for a fact that it is not only God who knows the worth of these precious Trisomy children. Yes, He knows it best because He created them, but I know the worth of these precious children also, because I was blessed to be the mom of one. Everyone who took the time to know Grace, to hold her, to see her, knew her worth. If they saw our family at school, at church, at the store, at the ballfield, they knew she was a valued member of our family. She was a precious gift who blessed us in so many ways every moment of every day.

The neurologist put Grace on her first seizure medicine that day. He ordered an EEG. He also scheduled Grace to be tested once again for full Trisomy 13. He wanted them to check all of her cells. Surely, in his mind, she was only partial Trisomy 13 because she was still alive and seemed to be doing quite well! The EEG proved that her brain was seizing in most sections. It was not centralized. The test for full or partial Trisomy 13, we would have to find out at our next visit. The medication seemed to keep her seizures under control for the first couple weeks.

By December 14, Grace started having diarrhea and a little vomiting. She was 14 lbs. and 1 oz. After about a week of diarrhea, we took her off her seizure medicine to see if that was the cause. Apparently not, because the diarrhea lasted another week and a half. By December 26, Grace had lost almost a pound. The doctors started testing all of her stools. By December 29 she was down to 12 lbs. 14 oz. They finally had enough diapers to test, but still couldn't figure out what she had. I was getting fearful once again, wondering if she was ever going to get better. Thankfully we had planned in the previous weeks that Grace would be dedicated to the Lord in a church service on December 30. We went forward with the plan. Rich and I dedicated her to the Lord. In reality we were dedicating ourselves to love her, raise her, and train her up to know Jesus and His Word. We were entrusting our little girl to the Lord. She was His child. The church body committed to support us in all the ways they were able. This was a very special day, a day that we didn't think we would have. As the church came together that day to pray for us, God answered our prayers once again and the diarrhea went away. I realize that most people may think, *"It's just diarrhea, something that goes away eventually, not something to be afraid of."* As I had read on the Trisomy website and message boards, I realized that little things like diarrhea are often big problems for these Trisomy kids. A case of the flu, pneumonia, or RSV (Respiratory Syncytial Virus) can take their lives so much more easily than a normal baby or child. I didn't feel like I was letting fear rule in my life, but when sickness came, fear seemed to creep in with it. On December 31, when our nurse came by the house to visit, Grace weighed 13 lbs. 7.5 oz.! She was gaining weight again and not dehydrated anymore.

***

I was doing better on some of my fears at that point. When Grace was still in her first few months, I was fearful driving by myself with just the two of us in the car. She always sat right behind me and I couldn't see her very well. Sometimes, when she was really quiet, I would fear that she would just pass away while I was driving. Or if I was driving with Grace while she was sick, I would worry that she would throw up in her seat and aspirate due to the angle of her seat. At the time, I didn't realize the fear my kids had either. Eric and Ethan were very good helpers and I was confident in having Ethan watch Grace for short periods of time if I had to run into the store or to the school to pick up someone. I knew that he knew what to do if she started spitting up. I had taught him to unbuckle her and sit her upright. One day I found him in tears and realized caring for Grace was too hard on him emotionally. After that day, I tried not to put him in that position again. I knew the fears I struggled with as a grown woman were difficult to live with. I couldn't even imagine the fears my sweet kids had with Grace. They loved her so much! They loved helping take care of her and holding her. Eric, Ethan, and Megan were the absolute sweetest children. I just kept praying that God would give them what they needed for this journey with Grace, always trying to point out God's goodness to us. He was indeed so good!

While Rich had been home for ten days over Christmas we were able to spend some time with family, but before we knew it, he had to go back to San Antonio. He was loving the weather there but missing us a lot as we missed him. It was such a crazy time trying to keep up with the three kids in school, in the AWANA program, and other church activities, as well as the boys both playing basketball. If I had not had such wonderful friends from church and school and my wonderful sister there to help me, I don't know how I would have accomplished it all. They helped with watching and transporting the kids, and pitched in with grocery shopping as well as cleaning and organizing my house so it would show well. Trying to sell a house with four kids is hard enough, but when you factor in the special needs of Grace, it was on a whole new level. Her medicines, suction machine, feeding supplies, and many other needs had to be ready to go out the door in a moment's notice. Grace was always having doctors' appointments and there were always nurses and different people in the house to help figure out her needs. We had finished hospice care by then, thank the Lord, as they'd finally decided that Grace's death was not imminent.

Through all the chaos, Grace stayed fairly healthy, which definitely helped. Rich was back to celebrate her first birthday in April! We had many family and friends over to celebrate. It was a wonderful time to share with everyone as well as a time to thank them for their many prayers, encouragement, and help. I made a "Sunshine" cake because Grace was my little sunshine! April was a great month celebrating Grace's birthday. To make it even better, our house finally sold! We were even blessed by our realtors. They had thought that two things were preventing our house from selling: the paint job in the upstairs bathroom and our dark, outdated kitchen cabinets. I simply did not have the energy or time to paint either space. Our sweet realtors came in on days we were gone and painted them both! Soon after that was done, we had our first offer. Right after that, I went down and helped Rich find us a home in San Antonio. We would have our family back together again soon. The kids and I missed Rich so much that thoughts of being back with him softened our sadness of leaving friends and family.

Before the move, Rich and I were blessed to take a trip to Puerto Vallarta together. It was a work trip, but his company was good enough to let spouses come and make a vacation of it! I was thankful that my mother and sister were willing to take on the task of taking care of the kids, even Grace. That was no small task. They had to learn the feeding tube, the medicines, and deal with Grace's lack of sleeping at night! The day before I flew out to meet Rich in Houston to go on our trip, Grace had her first laugh! I was changing her from her pajamas into her clothes and she had this quiet laugh. The sweetest thing I have ever heard. What a fun surprise before my trip, and a special blessing for my mom and sister as they heard it many more times while I was gone!

Rich and I had been apart for so long that it seemed like I had learned how to be a single mom and he had learned to do life without us. It was a huge blessing to be back together again. We had such a wonderful time on our trip that I didn't even worry about everyone at home. Immediately when I got home from the trip and Rich had gone back to San Antonio, I felt that longing in my heart. I missed him. I had been so busy in the previous months just trying to keep my head above water that I had forgotten what that was like. We had so much fun being together. I couldn't wait to get to San Antonio to be with him all the time.

Every day was packed with so much to do, it was unreal. I was incredibly stressed, but it would be over soon. We had class picnics, last days of school, final baseball games along with all the good-byes. Coaches for Eric, Ethan, and Megan were all trying to make deals with us to leave our kids to finish out the seasons!

Yes, our move back to Omaha in 2001 had definitely been God ordained. It was not for the reasons that I thought at the time, but for much bigger reasons. God knew exactly where we would receive the best help, encouragement, and support to make it through my pregnancy with Grace as well as the first year of her life. He knew exactly what doctors needed to see the miracle that she was and which doctor would be best for Grace in that first year of life. We could not have chosen any better. I will forever hold a special place in my heart for our friends and family who live in and around Omaha. They really stepped up and showed us God's love by their prayers, words, and actions. I loved them dearly and always will.

Wednesday, May 21, the house was packed up. I was so thankful that Rich's company took care of that for us. I just had to be there to supervise. Gracie and I spent our last night in the house alone, while Eric, Ethan, and Megan spent the night with their friends. Then the next day the truck came and it was loaded. What an exhausting day. Megan had her last day on Wednesday and the boys finished on Thursday at noon. They all went home with friends once again. So in the afternoon while Grace napped, I cleaned the house. As soon as the movers finished taking all the boxes and furniture out of a room, I was cleaning it. After that, I made the rounds to collect the kids and say our last good-byes. Then I drove with the kids to Grandpa and Grandma Lundt's farm in South Dakota where we would stay for the next two nights before we headed south to Texas.

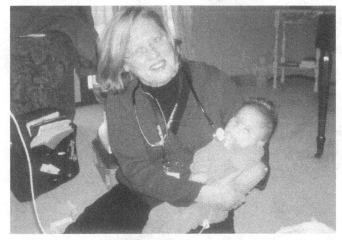

Hospice Nurse

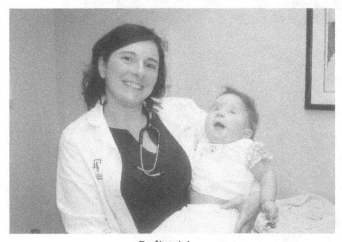

Pediatrician

Student Nurse holding Grace

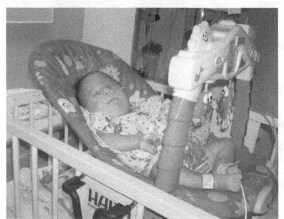

Grace in hospital

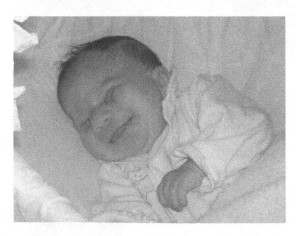

Grace smiling in the bassinet

Ready for a run in the jogging stroller

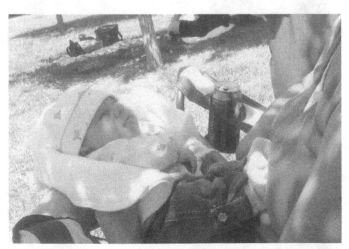

Grace at the ballfield

Professional pictures from Now I Lay Me Down To Sleep

4

God's Provision

Our move to San Antonio went smoothly. The kids had become good little travelers and were very helpful with Grace in the van. Grace was always an excellent traveler. Rich had been living in an apartment in San Antonio that was close to his hotel. While it had worked well for him, he was thankful to be moving back in with the family and to be home. I don't think either of us realized how long the commute would take for him to get to and from work each day, though. We had chosen a home on the northern end of San Antonio. At the time, it felt like we were closer to the country or in a small town. This fit us better than a home downtown closer to his hotel. We loved our new home and our new neighborhood. The house did not need to have a lot done to it except painting most of the rooms. At first, Rich and I thought that it would be a fun task to take on as a family. We soon realized that if we wanted to paint it all just once, he and I needed to do it without the kids. While they were enjoying painting, Rich and I were having to go back and do another layer over their paint job.

On June 5, an insurance man doing our home inspection came by the house. I had not been very quick to tell people about our miracle baby lately, but this nice man walked right into it. I just couldn't resist! He saw Grace sleeping in her chair and said, "She looks like a good healthy baby." I just had to chuckle to myself and then said, "Well, she looks good but she's not quite healthy." I explained Trisomy 13 and he asked what her prognosis was. I shared with him what our neurologist had said but added that only God really knew. He commented that if she dies, it's because God wants her there with Him. I agreed with him and assured him that it would be all right if the Lord called her to Him because I knew I would be going to heaven eventually also. The previous days in San Antonio, I had been getting frustrated that I could not find a good pediatrician and was also wishing I was still in Omaha because I knew of a Trisomy 13 baby that was about to be born in Lincoln, Nebraska. I wished I could have been there to support and help that family, but it wasn't in God's plan. So being able to share about what God was doing for our baby, even if it was with this stranger who I would probably never see again, was a reassurance to me that we were in San Antonio for God's reasons. I couldn't see them all yet, and I may not ever, but I could trust Him to provide our family's every need.

Our previous Omaha doctors and therapists had made some calls and given me phone numbers of people to get in touch with to get services going for Grace. We did not want to lose ground on her physical and occupational therapy. Thankfully those people fell into place quickly in San Antonio, and God also did provide the perfect pediatrician for Grace. Her office was nice and close to our home, and she had a very caring heart.

I took on the task of finding a church. We needed a church that would be like family because we were without any in Texas. I had grown to realize that just because Grace had been doing well for a while now, that was not a guarantee. *If* she were to get sick was not the question, but rather *when* she would get sick. I couldn't help wondering when she would have her first hospitalization in this new city. We would need help. I knew I would personally need support and encouragement. I had found our last few churches by looking for churches that had AWANA programs. The kids had always enjoyed AWANA, and I was hoping that they could finish going through the program. I knew that if they learned all that Scripture, it would stick with them when they needed it. So I made a call to the closest church to us that offered AWANA. It was just north of us in Bulverde, Texas. The lady who answered the phone was one of the church secretaries. She had a sweet southern accent and was so friendly. I asked a few questions about the church and then explained a little bit about our family, primarily focusing on our little special needs girl, Grace. Did this lady think that their church would be a good fit for us? She assured me that they were a very caring church and would love for us to come try them out. She said she would meet us the next Sunday before the service started and sit with us. So that is what we did! We all felt very welcomed there and liked the service, so we never visited another church. We very quickly found a new Christian school for the kids that was not too far from us, which was also in the small town of Bulverde. Staff, families, and children were all very welcoming at this small school. It did not take long at all to feel like this was home. The kids quickly made friends and were able to participate in athletics and music.

For the first month and a half, everything seemed to be coming together. We were finding the doctors and specialists who were needed for Grace. We were enjoying the neighborhood pool and going on walks, runs, and bike rides. We all enjoyed being outdoors. Many days I was feeling like I had victory in Christ on the journey I was on, days that were filled with peace, joy, and strength—the same words that God had given me to describe the day Grace was born! Yet there were other days, like July 6, when I felt overwhelmed with feelings of despair. I was worried that if I was not spiritually where I needed to be, God may decide to take Grace home. Yes, I was still reading God's Word, but I didn't feel as focused on Him as I had been in Omaha. I knew these feelings weren't God's truth. I knew that the number of Grace's days and God's purpose and plan for her life were totally unrelated to my Christian walk. I had struggled with the same feelings in the past and knew that they were lies from Satan. In the name of Jesus, I rejected those thoughts and tried to move on.

I had been a runner since junior high when my coach told me to run a mile a day through the summer and I would be ready for high school track. Well, that is what I did, and he was right! I had a really good track season my freshman year. Little did I know that the habit I started at the age of fourteen would have such an impact on my life. Yes, for years it would be a means to an end. I wanted to do well in track or volleyball, so I would run. I wanted to maintain a certain weight and be athletic, so I would run. I also just liked the muscular legs it gave me! In college, running was often a social time to talk with a friend. After I married, it became my time to talk with the Lord. I always had a praise song in my head, so in my mind I was either singing or praying while running. It was a time to cast all my cares on Him. It relieved me oftentimes of my stress and calmed me of my anxious heart. As I ran in the hot summer days of San Antonio, and yes, they were extremely hot, God reminded me that He had made me strong in Him to handle whatever would come.

By this time, Grace's tummy had become very red and raw around her feeding tube. There was always acidic drainage around it. She would cry from the pain it caused every time we would change the bandage on it, but we did our best to make it better by always putting powder on it with bandages to protect it. During my runs, I would praise and thank God for the many good things in our lives. God gave me the patience and strength each day to continue changing those bandages and to comfort Grace through it. It was not easy to see our baby suffer and hurt. God was giving me peace each night as I laid her down to bed and I would say out loud every night, "She's Yours, Lord. You made her and I trust You will watch over her and protect her through the night. I give her to You and I trust You."

My journal for July 16, 2008, read: "Yes, I am truly thankful for God's perfect little creation in Grace. According to the world, she has many anomalies, imperfections, and health issues, but in God's eyes and mine, she is perfect and so beautiful."

***

In the middle of July when we were just beginning to make a change in Grace's seizure medications, Grace suffered a new type of seizure. I didn't even see the first one that she had. I was downstairs working in the kitchen while Grace was up in Megan's room and the kids were playing with her when all of a sudden, Ethan came running to the top of the stairs. He was crying and yelling for me and saying something. I couldn't understand any of it except for Grace's name. I went running up the stairs but was too late to see what had happened. Ethan tried to tell me what happened but was too shaken up to even explain it. I knew it must have been a different kind of seizure, because her jerks weren't that alarming to the kids anymore. Later, when Ethan was calm, I had him show me exactly what he saw. He held his arms out to the sides and shook them. My poor Ethan, I knew it had scared him. He loved his baby sister so much.

Two days later, I saw for myself exactly what Ethan had seen. It lasted for about ten seconds and Grace was quite agitated when she came out of it. She was talking and waving her arms around. I just picked her up, held her, and cried. These episodes happened two more times within the week, although there could have been more that I didn't see. One of them happened at a time when the radio was playing the familiar song, "Walking Her Home" by Mark Schultz. It had only been a couple of weeks since I had heard of a two-year-old Trisomy 13 child who had died. He had seven seizures in one day, and the last one had taken his life. I was really struggling again with the thought of losing Grace. I had struggled a lot with that thought through her first year of life. It had been a rough first year with many medical emergencies and the hospice team ever so present. I thought I had finally reached victory for the most part in that area in the last couple of months, but here I found myself struggling all over again, and I had been struggling all week. Fear and anxiety were very present in my heart. As the song played, I danced with Grace around our kitchen, trying so hard to enjoy the moment of loving her. As I did, God reminded me of the two words He had given me during my pregnancy, "Hold loosely." But as I danced and thought of those words, I held Grace so tightly. I knew God was trying to remind me that she was His. I was fearful that He was trying to prepare me for what may happen in the coming months, just as He had prepared me for the move by telling me to get my house ready to sell, and just as He had put many special needs kids in my path during my pregnancy as a way of preparing me for Grace.

This fear was trying to overtake me, not just the fear of the seizures, but also what our new neurologist had recently told me. He'd said that Trisomy 13 kids don't live into double digit numbers. Either by a viral infection or by their brain not functioning correctly, they pass away. Living in the heat of San Antonio also made me realize that Grace's brain did not regulate her body temperature. She did not sweat! If and when she got a fever or got overheated, she had more seizures. Whenever I thought about losing Grace, about the day when she would die and go home to heaven, the words *destruction* and *destroying* immediately came into my mind as I thought about what would happen to me. I had mental pictures twice of what Grace would look like when she died or how I would carry her at that moment. This is not how I believe God wanted me to respond in that very moment or when the time of her death came. I know God was working in my heart, and this was a struggle I would work through for the months, even years, to come. I recall going on my run many times through our San Antonio neighborhood and just coming to a complete stop because I was so broken down in tears, crying out to God. Each time this happened He would pick me up, turn my eyes back on Him, because He was who I could trust in. He would get me running again. He would help me finish strong. God was giving me this perfect picture of my life. Grace's death would seem like it was too much to bear, but

He would pick me up, set my eyes on Him, get me running again, and help me to finish strong.

Grace was His perfectly created child, created for His glory and honor. Her days were in His hands and His control, just as Scripture tells us. Nothing I did, or didn't do, would prolong Grace's life. Satan was trying to rob me of the joy of having her with me right there in that moment and also attempting to steal the focus off of giving God the glory.

My prayer in my journal: "Lord God, please allow me to focus on You and Your plan once again for the life of this very special baby."

A friend reminded me of Jesus's words in John 10:10, "The thief comes only to steal and kill and destroy; I have come that they may have life, and might have it to the full." And He said in Romans 8:6, "The mind of sinful man is death, but the mind controlled by the Spirit is life and peace."

I thanked the Lord for bringing me back around to life and peace. I prayed that God would please show my children that same peace. On August 1, Ethan was lying next to Grace on the couch when he told me, "When I get big, I'm going to cure T13 and also make blind people see." Then he turned to Grace and said, "I'm going to start with you." Shortly after that he had tears in his eyes because Grace had been coughing. He said she was choking, turning red, and not breathing. I hated when he got so frightened but seemed unable to encourage him not to worry so much. God is the only one who is truly able to take away our fears.

Poor little Gracie had been sick since July 16 with a cold, cough, and raspy breathing. It was mostly in her upper airway (throat). She would spike a fever for one day about once a week. This would last for the next couple of months. First, she had an ear infection and got her first antibiotic; then another one-day fever, so we tried a second antibiotic. Then yet another fever for Tuesday, Wednesday, and Friday. We went into our pediatrician's office once again and she sent us for x-rays this time. They said it was pneumonia and gave Grace two antibiotic shots in her legs. Then we were sent home on our third antibiotic. On day eight of being on the antibiotic, Grace spiked a fever again. I took her to the ER thinking the pneumonia must be getting worse. They did blood work and a chest x-ray. The x-ray of her lungs looked really good and clear. The blood work, however, showed a high white blood cell count, which led them to test for a urinary tract infection. Grace had a UTI that grew into a nasty infection, which is usually only treated by IV antibiotics. They gave her antibiotics at the ER and sent us home on yet another antibiotic. Later they changed it to yet another antibiotic. By September 18, the UTI was cleared up. Grace's breathing was still quite raspy. It just sounded like a rattle or gurgling noise in the back of her throat. By this time, we had nursing care at the house on some days. I was very thankful for the extra set of ears listening to Grace's lungs and checking her vitals. I was not the only one keeping my eyes on Grace anymore. Our nurse was wonderful and very loving and attentive to Grace. It definitely gave me peace of mind knowing she was there. I could choose to go to activities at school with the kids, get cleaning done, get a much-needed nap, run out shopping, or even get my running done for the day.

On Tuesday, September 23, 2008, Grace had an appointment with her pulmonary specialist. The nurse practitioner there said that Grace's lungs sounded good. Grace had sounded good when she was asleep but was still very rattly when she was awake. The pulmonary specialist told us that it wasn't a lung issue but a neurological issue. I knew it! It had been like that ever since we had switched seizure medications. The nurse practitioner said that Grace had a pool of water at the bottom of her throat and we needed to decrease her seizure medications. We had been using the suction machine many times throughout each day to try to relieve Grace of the many secretions, but they just constantly pooled up more each time. I felt horrible for having to do it so much knowing that it could be very irritating on her throat and the back of her mouth. Finally, on Friday, we were able to get permission from her neurologist to lower the amount of medication.

By Sunday, Grace sounded better! Then, on Monday, she sounded a bit raspy again. Figuring out the right amounts of all her medications and inhalers was going to be a bit tricky. I prayed that God would give me the wisdom to know how to take care of Grace so she could be as healthy as possible and enjoy her life to its fullest. The decrease in medication also helped Grace be awake more and she was smiling more again. What a blessing!

By October, Grace was having constant urinary tract infections (UTIs). The pediatrician sent us to a urologist who wanted to get some testing done on Grace's bladder and kidneys, so into the children's hospital we went on October 10. They did a renal ultrasound and a VCUG. These tests would show her kidney status and bladder function. The test showed that Grace was refluxing from her bladder. I didn't even know this was possible! It also showed that Grace's kidneys were not normal. This was exactly why I would get nervous every time we went to a new specialist and looked closely at a new body part. There was always something "not normal." As I left the hospital with my sweet girl that day, I wondered and worried what this new diagnosis would mean for our girl.

I went from there to Grace's next appointment, which was her eighteen-month checkup at her pediatrician's office. We obviously had not been with this doctor's office long enough for everyone to know us yet. I signed in and the receptionist handed me an eighteen-month developmental questionnaire. Instantly I thought, *"You've got to be kidding me."* I will admit that I was already feeling a bit emotional from the hospital experience, but I started filling out the questionnaire anyway. I started circling all the No's. No, she was not walking. No, she was not sitting on her own. No, she had not started crawling. No, she could not point to her body parts. No, she could not hold a cup or stack blocks. I put "Not Applicable" next to the ones requiring sight. Halfway through the questionnaire, I could feel the floodgates of tears getting ready to come. Finally, I put a big X on the last group of questions and handed it back to the receptionist. I am sure she did not have a clue what she had done, and certainly did not do it on purpose. Determined to pull myself together and love Gracie for exactly who she was, I picked Grace up out of her pink stroller and held her very close. Then I got her rattle out of the diaper bag and put it in her hand. I had worked on this with her before, but never got any response from Grace. So far she hadn't tried to shake the rattle on her own. I started our routine where I took her little hand in mine, helping her hold the rattle, and said, "Shake, shake, shake . . . shake, shake the rattle." I helped her do this several times. Then I put it in her hand one more time, making sure each finger was gripping it. I let go and said, "Shake, shake, shake . . . shake, shake the rattle." And she did! I did it several times more to make sure it wasn't a fluke, and she kept doing it! Even the lady across the waiting room said, "She's doing it!" I was so proud of Grace and thankful that God gave us that moment! He saw my brokenness in that moment and met my need at that time. He was reminding me that Grace was absolutely perfect just as He created her to be, whether the boxes on the questionnaire were marked Yes or No.

When we were called in to the doctor's office, the receptionist came in to apologize. Grace weighed 24 lbs. and was 32 in. long. The doctor had received the kidney report so I asked her what the abnormal part meant in the report. She skirted around a bit as she explained and then threw out the words "renal failure." A big red flag went off in my mind and I immediately said, "Is that the same as kidney failure? People die from that, right? Is that a sure thing or are you speculating?" Our sweet doctor right away tried to take back what she had said, claiming that we needed to talk to the kidney specialist first to get clarity.

Leaving the doctor's office, I felt absolutely crushed once again and was desperate to find out what this all meant. I went home and over the next two days I went on message boards, the internet, and asked questions of every doctor and person in the medical field that I could. Later, I realized I was asking the wrong questions. My papers from the doctor said "echogenic kidneys," which is a very vague diagnosis, so I was not getting any specific answers.

On October 11, I went on a run in our neighborhood. Once again, I was crying out to my Lord. I wanted answers so badly that I couldn't think of anything else. I wanted to know what all of this meant for Grace's future and I didn't want to wait until November 5 for the appointment with the nephrologist (kidney specialist). In my tears and talking to the Lord, He simply told me that I did not need to understand Grace's kidneys yet, He would let me know in His time and I could trust Him. He was Grace's Creator and had made her perfect. He did not make any mistakes and her days were completely in His hands. My understanding her kidneys would not lengthen her days. Once again God gave me the incredible peace that passes all understanding. He gave me joy and contentment again as I kept putting my worries in His hands.

Philippians 4:6–7, "Do not be anxious about anything, but in everything, by prayer and petition, with thanksgiving, present your requests to God. And the peace of God, which transcends all understanding, will guard your hearts and your minds in Christ Jesus."

***

On Monday, October 13, Megan, Grace, and I went to visit a new friend. We had learned of a Trisomy 13 family in the San Antonio area. Their child was four years old. She was absolutely beautiful! It was so good to talk with a family who could understand and relate to everything we were going through. Their sweet little girl was sitting up on the floor with perfect head control watching fun little musical DVDs. She would smile and laugh and get all excited because she knew exactly what song was coming next. She tapped her daddy's lips when she wanted him to sing along! It was so encouraging to see them. I left their house feeling that yes, I could do this and I really wanted to do this!

On October 29, we went to the urologist. He looked at the tests that had been done on Grace's bladder and kidneys. He explained the possibility of surgery for her reflux and put her on yet another medication to help prevent her from getting the UTIs that still seemed to be a constant battle. Grace had been born with a crooked tushy crack. No one had ever said anything about it, and I actually thought it was quite adorable. He noticed it and said that he wanted an MRI done on her spine. He thought that it was a sign that her spine could be tethered down or there could even be a tumor there putting pressure on the kidneys and bladder. As much as I didn't want to find out any more problems, I knew it would be good to get things figured out to stop the UTIs. He also wanted us to see a neurosurgeon soon to do more testing. Every week it seemed like it was something new.

Philippians 4:13, "I can do everything through him who gives me strength."

November 5 finally came along with the appointment to the nephrologist. This was a tough appointment. Some days I wished that we lived in the time where they couldn't figure out *every* problem in your body. I know that they still can't totally, but this much knowledge is hard to know. The nephrologist said that Grace had some hydronephrosis (water in her kidneys) but not a worrisome amount yet. She said that Grace's kidneys were bigger than they should be, the tissue was bad, especially in the right kidney, and there should be an outer and inner part of the kidney that can be visibly seen as different. Grace's all looked the same. She told us that Grace was headed for renal (kidney) failure. It could be in five years, or Grace could surprise us and make it to her teens. She said that Grace must have some "good kidney" in reserve that her body was using otherwise she would not be growing as well as she was. Then she told us that it would be her job to protect the good kidney by keeping it healthy and stopping the UTIs. Before I left the office that day, I asked the doctor what renal failure looked like. Was it quick, slow, painful? She answered, "Well, it's not quick, but people pray to die this way. The poison gets in the blood sedating the brain. So they don't feel any pain and just go to sleep." At this point in our conversation nothing could possibly sound good.

This was a very difficult day with very hard news to hear. Then, to top it off, we arrived home to a message on the answering machine that Grace had yet another UTI. I had always known that her life expectancy was not the longest, but nothing she had so far had seemed life-threatening. Now we knew what most likely would take our precious Grace's life—kidney failure. Once again, I felt totally crushed and heartbroken. The tears just kept coming.

My journal: "Lord God, I need your peace and strength so much. I would so much rather live the rest of my life in doctor's offices and ER's and hospitals with Grace here, than to live a 'normal' life with her gone. People act like it must be so hard to live with all this 'medical stuff' going on all the time, but my biggest and only struggle is the thought of losing her. My biggest comfort right now is knowing that God will give me what I need when I need it."

My grandmother passed away that November. I was blessed that Rich was able to take off work and drive us all back to Iowa for the funeral. While it was a sad occasion, it was a blessing to be reminded of the wonderful grandmother she had been as well as the godly heritage that had been passed down to me through my family. I received so much love and encouragement from my aunts, uncles, and cousins. My uncle and my brother, who are both pastors, did the memorial service and the funeral service. My brother's message especially touched me as he pointed out the many hard things that my grandmother had faced in her life and that with God's help, she had made it through. She had faced the Great Depression. She had taken care of my grandfather for many years as he suffered from ALS. She cared for him to the end and then had the big task of being a single parent to their eight children. She went through the hardships of growing old herself. She did all of this while giving to many others constantly who were in need. She was very giving. Our time there was short, but also so sweet as I watched my other grandmother hold Grace in her arms. The trip was a quick one, but I returned to San Antonio rejuvenated and refreshed. I would be able to handle whatever God sends our way, with His help.

We were also blessed in November by having two different families come to visit us. Both were like family to us, and both were such a blessing. They were reminders that we did have friends, and that God would provide us with friends in this new place. We had friends who prayed for us, friends who encouraged us, and friends who had held us up when we needed it. Distance and time apart do not seem to matter when you have friends in Christ. They are truly family as God's Word says.

On November 26, Grace and I had a busy day. Her first appointment was at 9:00 a.m. with the urologist. He confirmed that Grace did indeed have a tethered spinal cord. This meant that Grace's spinal cord was abnormally attached to the tissues around the spine. As a result, the spinal cord could not move freely around within the spinal canal. The urologist wanted us to schedule an appointment with a neurosurgeon as well as do more tests that he was certain the neurosurgeon would want to have done. So everything was scheduled and Grace and I drove to our next appointment across town with the neurologist. Grace's seizures were continuing to change, so he continued changing her medication. The seizures had changed from the myoclonic jerks to the arms shaking, and now they had changed to her arms and legs going stiff. These were the worst kind so far, but they didn't seem to leave Grace as agitated as the previous ones had. In fact, she seemed to come out of them quite happily sometimes. The new medication soon changed the seizures back to myoclonic jerks. As we spoke with the neurologist, I updated him on all of Grace's other new findings with her bladder, spinal cord, and kidneys. On our way out the door, he tried to encourage me by saying, "You're doing all you can for her." I knew this was true, but it left me with the realization that no matter how much I did, it would never be enough.

***

On Friday, December 6, Grace had a fever and started throwing up and having diarrhea. I took her to our pediatrician who sent us on to the ER. Grace was dehydrated. Her bi-carb count should have been between 22 and 26, but Grace's was at 16. They said that if it was 15, they would have to admit her. Since it was 16, I could choose if I wanted her admitted or if I wanted to bring her back the next day to be poked again and re-checked. I hated to have to bring her back to be poked again, but Rich was in Houston with work until late that night. I had to pick up the kids from school, and Eric had a basketball game. So I chose to bring her home and told the ER team we would be back on Saturday. Saturday came and Grace was not any better. I knew she would be admitted, so I tried to get a lot done that morning, preparing food for the family, getting laundry done, and packing for her and me, because I was not sure how long we would be in the hospital. Her bi-carb count was still at 16, so she was admitted right away. They had tested her for everything and finally decided it was just a stomach virus. Ethan and Eric had the same sickness at home. Poor Rich had sick duty for the weekend with them. They allowed us to come home on Monday, December 8, but Grace continued gagging for a week. I wasn't sure she was truly over the virus.

On Tuesday, December 16, Grace had her tests done for the neurosurgeon. This time the bladder ultrasound showed no hydronephrosis! Praise the Lord! The other test, a video urodynamics test, showed a Grade 2 reflux from her bladder that was reaching the kidneys. He said we might consider surgery for the reflux but for now wanted to just try a bladder relaxant. He was surprised to hear of Grace's kidney problems. He thought they had looked pretty good and wondered how the kidney specialist had come up with her prognosis. How confusing this all was! How can two highly trained specialists look at the exact same tests and come up with totally different views on the severity of an issue?

On Thursday, December 18, Grace again ran a fever, threw up, and had lots of diarrhea again. I knew we were headed back into the hospital. I quickly got us packed, cleaned up the house, and did laundry once again while the nurse took care of Grace. We left for the ER and were admitted again. One blessing of using the same ER over and over is that they start to know you. We never had to sit in the waiting area with the many other sick children. We were quickly moved to a quieter, less contagious space. They ran more tests to make sure they had not missed anything from our previous visit. It was very late by the time we got to our room. I was hoping for the same quick progression that we'd had our previous stay, but this time the doctors decided to take things much slower. Every time Grace got a virus with vomiting and diarrhea, they had to shut off her feeds that went in through her feeding tube, empty her stomach, and then slowly introduce her back to just Pedialyte, and then gradually do ¾ Pedialyte to ¼ formula, then ½ Pedialyte to ½ formula, then ¼ Pedialyte to ¾ formula, and finally back to full formula. On Saturday, we were just getting ready to go to ½ strength Pedialyte and ½ strength formula when Grace started gagging and threw up again. We had to shut off her feeds completely and start all over at emptying her stomach.

While I felt absolutely awful for Grace, I also felt awful for my other three kids. They were only six-, nine-, and eleven-years old. It seemed like I was missing so many days and nights with them. I had missed their Christmas program and parties at school the day before. I could easily go down the "mom-guilt" road with all that I was missing with Eric, Ethan, and Megan when I was with Grace in the hospital, but I could just not bear to leave her alone. Grace was only one-and-a-half years old! I could only imagine how frightening it was for her to find herself in a foreign place with strange voices of people she did not know and could not see. I thought too of all the needle pokes into her arms, legs, feet, and toes that she so patiently endured, as well as all the other invasive tests that she couldn't see coming! She couldn't speak up if needed. Who would tell them that they had already poked there, or that sometimes the IV went in best down in her foot, or that she had prosthetic eyes while they shined their little light in them as if they had perhaps not read her chart very well? At least if I was there holding her hand, hopefully she would feel safe. She could hear my voice giving her reassurances that she was not alone.

The days of December were going by quickly and I was not ready for Christmas at all. I wasn't sure when I would be, because there was no end in sight to this hospitalization. I had managed to bring some material to make Megan a blanket and did actually get that finished while in the hospital with Grace. It was one of those fleece tie blankets. I had made a red one for Eric one year, then a blue one for Ethan the next year. Megan's would be made out of her favorite colors, one side green and one side blue. I wondered whether it might be the only thing I would get done for Christmas. Thankfully on Sunday, December 21, two friends from our church came to the hospital to visit Grace. While they were there, our Sunday school teacher called with instructions for me to make a shopping list. She wanted me to send it and a credit card back with these friends to give to her. I did. Then on Monday, she and another lady from our Sunday school class did all of my Christmas shopping! Everything on my list was bought! How incredible for God to be so good and for them to bless us in that way!

I kept telling the doctors at the hospital that it was our goal to be home before Christmas, and thankfully they did their best. I was not sure we should have really gone home, because right after I signed the discharge papers on Christmas Eve, Grace threw up in our hospital room. I was so worried that the doctor may change her mind, but she gave instructions to shut off Grace's feeds for a couple hours and to try not to be back in the hospital again that year. We made it home Christmas Eve! Rich watched Grace for a few hours while I ran around getting food for Christmas dinner and we managed to have the Christmas that we had hoped to have. We were all home! Rich's mom and two brothers would make it to visit us for Christmas that year also.

The worst part of our hospital stay was that Grace's sleep schedule got all messed up, because the nurses and doctors came in at all sorts of crazy times. Grace and I would finally get to bed between 12:00

a.m. and 1:30 a.m., and then they would come for rounds by 5:30 a.m. Usually Grace and I would be napping again by 8:00 or 8:30 a.m. Of course, this sleep schedule came home with Grace. Even though the stay was longer than I had wanted, I tried to keep the perspective that we were only in for a stomach virus. It was nothing more serious. I was thankful that Rich was able to take care of the older three kids. Families from school and church helped Rich with the kids and also with meals. God was very good to put us in this place with this school and church. We did not return to the hospital that year!

***

On January 7, Grace had an appointment with the neurosurgeon about her spine. The doctor was very thorough getting all of Grace's history and checking Grace over. She told me that Grace had scoliosis, definitely had a tethered spine, but also had a lot of spinal fluid, which was a big concern for her. She could not see where the excess fluid was coming from. So she ordered yet another MRI and CT scan of Grace's spine and brain. The L4 segment on her spine was also very low, which was concerning. The doctor had many other concerns but would give her recommendation after the next tests were done. She wanted to know if the excess fluid came down from the brain due to some malformation. *Had she not heard me tell her that the brain malformation was gone, did not exist?* It was another hard day. Once again, new doctors, new body parts looked at closely, and new things that were not normal in my sweet Grace's body. Regardless of the tests saying how abnormal my girl was, I knew with all my heart that she was made perfect in God's eyes.

Later that week while I was on a run, God reminded me that He did not just make Grace perfect, but He also made me perfect. He created me strong enough physically, spiritually, emotionally, and mentally so I could do this. It was okay that some days I cried, and I cried a lot! It was okay that some days I could not seem to focus on anything but Grace. He gave me feelings, longings, and desires and I am supposed to cry out to Him with all of my praises as well as my hurts and longings. I praise Him that He chose me to be her mom! He chose me to be by her side for every doctor's visit, every therapy session, every ER visit, every hospital stay, every needle poke, every IV poke, every x-ray and MRI, every long test, every procedure, and every surgery. I also got the privilege of seeing her many beautiful smiles, hearing her sweet breathy laugh, watching her grow stronger, and understand things like "kiss, kiss" and "head up," and listening to her steady breathing as she slept peacefully. Praise God!

On January 22, the MRI and tests had been completed, so with Rich by my side, we went to the surgeon's office to hear the results and her recommendations for surgery. To my dismay, she had us meet with her partner. I didn't even catch his name, but he did nothing but upset and frustrate me. His first question was "What's her prognosis?" I couldn't believe it. He had barely looked at her. I felt like saying, *"Her initial prognosis was five minutes, but they were obviously wrong."* Instead I calmly and graciously explained the kidney prognosis we had recently received and said Grace could live to be five or six years old or may surprise us and make it into her teens. The surgeon then went on to say that Grace's scoliosis was not that bad. He said her spinal cord was definitely tethered and was quite thick. He said they did not find any more problems with the brain or the spine. I felt like he was looking for something bad so he could just not do anything for Grace. Instead he said, "If she were a normal child, I would definitely say she needs the surgery to untether the cord, but I will let you two decide." He also said that he couldn't guarantee that she would ever stand or walk. We already knew that was not probable. That was not why we were needing the surgery. We needed it to take the pressure off the kidneys and the bladder. We needed to try to protect her from further kidney damage. Frustration beyond belief! Anger! I needed the Lord to lead us to a better doctor or at least to a better surgeon.

Later, on my run I was able to calm down, regain my perspective, and think through my many praises.

-Grace's scoliosis was not so bad.

-There were no other problems found on her spine or brain.

-It was God's plan to find this at this time. He would lead us to the right doctor at the right time to fix it.

-God is faithful and good.

Rich and I decided that the surgery needed to be done. We knew sooner would be better but decided to wait until June when my sister was planning to come for a visit. She would be very helpful with the other kids, and at that time Rich's job was just too stressful for him to get away for long periods of time. I prayed that the Lord would protect Grace's kidneys and bladder until the surgery could be done. We, along with many others, were praying also for God to fix her spine. I had just been encouraged that week in my Bible study to "Think Big!"

"If you can?" said Jesus. "Everything is possible for him who believes"
(Mark 9:23).

"Never be afraid to trust an unknown future to an all-knowing God."
—CORRIE TEN BOOM

Through January and February, Grace had a lot of sicknesses. Most of them couldn't be diagnosed so the doctors kept saying they were viral illnesses. It was two months of many fevers, seizures, vomiting, and diarrhea. It felt like we were constantly playing a huge guessing game. We also had to factor in the other kids' illnesses. They were sick way more often than usual. I think we were adjusting to the new state we were living in. There were new allergies to battle, the constant switch from hot to cold weather and then back again, as well as the many germs that came home from school. Megan was sick with croup, cough, troubles breathing, and fever also. Grace seemed to hold her own through it all. Her weight stayed the same at 24 lbs. 11 oz., but she was getting really long now. In the midst of it, though, we still saw her smiles and laughs occasionally and that blessed us all so much!

We kept busy with the numerous appointments. Grace's support team was up to nine doctors and specialists by then. She also had a physical therapist, an occupational therapist, and a speech therapist coming to the house, adding about eight visits to the house each week. They were all fabulous! I had not realized how tight Grace's little body had been all of those months. They stretched her, exercised her, and challenged her. All of these wonderful people, including the nurses who came a few days or nights each week to our home, became Grace's team, all working to help her enjoy life to the fullest and reach her fullest potential. They became like family, sharing in our tears and joy. We loved each and every one of them.

Some people may think that if you have a child with this many medical needs, you would have to really limit the activities your other children were able to participate in. That was not so with us. We wanted each of our kids to be able to enjoy their youth to the fullest. Why would we stop them from doing the activities they loved? Having a special needs sister put extra anxiety on them as it was. I didn't want them resenting her because they were suddenly being told that they couldn't play their sports or go to birthday parties. Eric, Ethan, and Megan did them all, it seemed. Football for the boys, basketball for all three of them, track for Eric, church activities, Math Olympics, speech meets, junior cheerleading for Megan, birthday parties, and overnights. We were really quite busy, and Grace was there enjoying it all too. She was very well known at the Christian school where the kids went as well as at church. She helped me cheer them on and she loved being out and about. I remember our first summer of Vacation Bible School at church. Grace and I would drop in to watch during worship time. The kids would be singing so loud with the worship team up front. On one of those special days, Grace raised her arms up into the air, praising Jesus all on her own. Many times previously I would lift her arms up in the air and say, "Praise Jesus, Gracie." On this day, with the kids praising Jesus and having so much fun with their song, Grace did it all by herself!

***

March 2009 proved to be another month that was tough but brought growth. We had just planned to have Grace's GJ tube replaced on March 11. Once again, God had other plans. On the night of March 3, our night nurse told me that Grace's feeding tube was not working. She couldn't get anything through it, so she'd shut Grace's feeds off. The next morning, I waited a couple hours before trying to turn her feeds on again. When I did, it worked fine. Then later that morning, I was going to give Grace a bath. I was about to put her in the bathtub when I noticed that her feeding tube was hanging out way farther than it should. I knew from past experience that it was important to keep the feeding tube in so the hole in her abdomen would stay open, so I pushed it back in as best as I could and taped it down to her tummy. Into her car seat in the van she went and off to the ER once again. Although it was a much farther drive, I loved our children's hospital in San Antonio. They knew Grace and got her in quickly once again. We had to wait six hours for Grace's tummy to be empty so she could be sedated and have the radiologist go in to make sure her tube was placed correctly. After they switched out her GJ tube, they told me that the tube had actually been in the right place. I guess I'd pushed it in correctly this time! God worked it all out because He knew it needed to be done. His timing is always best even if we don't know why at the time.

Then, on March 11, the day that had been scheduled for the GJ tube replacement which now was cancelled, we were in our pediatrician's office getting Grace checked out for yet another UTI. While we were there, the doctor heard a heart murmur. She listened and listened, and then had another person listen to be sure. Yes, there was a heart murmur. She had connections with a cardiologist and made a call right away for us. Yes, I started tearing up in the doctor's office. I tried my best to hold the tears in, but I just could not bear the thought of one more thing wrong with Grace. We were already planning on her surgery for her tethered spinal cord in the summer. We could not do yet another surgery, this time on her heart, and we just could not keep on finding "one more thing!" I cried all the way to school and tried to hide it from the kids when I picked them up. I didn't want them worrying about things that I didn't even know yet. I called a good friend on the drive to pray for me and God provided the peace that I needed.

They scheduled an appointment for that next Friday, only two days to wait. For the next two days I prayed and prayed and prayed that the murmur would be a minor problem that could be fixed easily. I was not sure Rich would be on board for another big surgery in addition to the spinal surgery in June. He was very stressed with this new job.

The day of her appointment came and Grace received a very thorough checkup from the cardiologist. He checked her blood pressures in her arms and legs, and found her arms were high and her legs were low. Then he did an EKG and an ultrasound of her heart. The doctor was so good. He was obviously not concerned about treating a child with Trisomy 13. Grace was supposed to lie still, but of course she wanted to kick and play, so the doctor started singing "The Wheels on the Bus" to Grace to calm her down. After all the tests, he told us that Grace's mitral valve was too thick and leaking blood back in the wrong direction, and that was causing the murmur. The bigger problem was her coarctation of the aorta, another diagnosis. Her aorta was too narrow in one spot, pushing most of her blood to her upper body, causing high blood pressure which is bad for . . . you'll never guess . . . the kidneys. It also was preventing much blood flow to her lower body, causing low blood pressure in her legs and hardly any pulse in her legs. This also was causing lack of blood flow to … guess what … the kidneys and bladder.

He told me that the aorta needed to be fixed before the spinal surgery. It would be a procedure, not a surgery! They would put a catheter in through an artery in her leg and go up to the aorta, inflate the balloon one to three times until the aorta was the desired size, and then they would take the balloon out. This procedure would help the blood flow, the high blood pressure, and possibly even lessen the mitral valve leakage. The doctor kept apologizing that it hadn't been detected sooner, as if it was his fault. He had never seen Grace until that day! I just smiled and said, "It's okay, it's not your fault." I was actually rejoicing on the inside, because God had heard my cries and answered in a big way. God just kept on answering our prayers and I just couldn't praise Him enough!

Psalm 116:1–2, "I love the LORD, for he heard my voice; he heard my cry for mercy. Because he turned his ear to me, I will call on him as long as I live."

It would not be a major surgery. Grace would possibly be in the hospital overnight, not too long. Even though it sounded like a difficult and perhaps scary procedure, I was so grateful that I could see God's hand in it all. He made her and once again showed Himself more than capable to care for her every need. I was also grateful for such a gentle, caring cardiologist. I totally trusted him to do it well.

Psalm 33:4–5, "For the word of the Lord is right and true; he is faithful in all he does. The Lord loves righteousness and justice; the earth is full of his unfailing love."

"We do not understand the intricate pattern of the stars in their courses, but we know that He who created them does, and that just as surely as He guides them, He is charting a safe course for us."
—BILLY GRAHAM

Yes, I could have chosen to be angry that this heart issue was just now detected. He said it would have developed soon after birth, and Grace was almost two years old! I couldn't count how many times and how many different nurses and doctors had listened to her heart or how many times they tried for a blood pressure. They very seldom got good blood pressures and would either quit trying or they would give some reason why her blood pressure wasn't right. Or they would take it in the leg and not be too concerned about the low reading. Was it because Grace was Trisomy 13? Did some of them hear the heart murmur and just not think she was worth asking the questions to check on something so important? There were so many opportunities for this heart condition to have been found and yet God chose to wait and reveal it at this time. He could have protected her kidneys by having it found earlier. I did not understand but was going to choose to trust again in His perfect timing and plan. Holding on to bitterness, anger, or trying to pass blame would not be beneficial for anyone. In the end, God knew, and this was His plan for Grace.

We were blessed in the middle of March when my dad, a farmer in Iowa, flew down to visit us for a week! I never would have guessed that my dad would fly at all, much less by himself. My mother had been sick for a while and there was no way she was able to come. If he didn't come before April, he wouldn't be able to later because planting season was approaching. It was so great having him in San Antonio with us. He went to Grandparent's Day at school with the kids. They loved it, and he really enjoyed seeing our great school. Dad had a very special bond with Grace. He would wake up early every morning because he knew she woke up early, usually by 5:00 a.m. I would get Grace out of bed and take her downstairs so she would not wake the others with her chatter. I always found my dad waiting for her. He would sit and hold her in those early hours, talking to her, singing to her, loving her. It was a very special time for both of them, but also for me. Even though many times I would go back to bed and get more sleep, I saw the joy that was going on between those two, and it gave me much joy. My dad would do that every time he visited us, as well as every time we visited the farm. My dad is a man who loves the simple things in life. He doesn't need to go sightseeing or eat at fabulous restaurants.

He loved taking the kids to the park with me, going on walks, eating at Beefy's Backyard Burger place. It was such a blessing to have him with us and, as always, hard to say good-bye.

***

March 30, 2009, was heart procedure day. Even though it was just a procedure and not surgery, I was anxious and worried that I may lose Grace during this. One of our home health nurses had told me she was worried that Grace would not make it through the procedure, and that comment definitely added to my worries. I found myself the week before trying to find someone who could professionally take Grace's picture. It hadn't been done since she was fifteen months old and I wanted something more recent if we lost her. I know the thought was morbid, but as I said before, Grace's death never escaped my mind for long. I found someone, but Grace unfortunately was wanting to sleep and would not smile for the pictures.

The procedure was done quite early in the morning at Children's Methodist Hospital in San Antonio. Rich was there with me as well as our pastor from church. I was very anxious, but Rich was just as calm as could be. He kept telling me I had nothing to worry about, that Grace was tough. He was right. I just didn't understand how he could remain so calm. They finished the procedure earlier than expected. They had inflated the balloon twice and were quite pleased with the improvement in the size of the aorta. Her blood pressure levels improved greatly also! I was amazed at the weight that seemed to immediately come off my shoulders as soon as I saw her. I didn't realize how worried I really was.

Grace came out of the anesthesia and was acting like her normal self. The challenge was keeping her legs down to make sure the bleeding stopped. She was happy and ready to kick all afternoon! I stood beside her bed holding her legs. It was an amazingly quick recovery, and Grace was able to go home the next morning.

On April 2, we had another appointment with the nephrologist. This time she said that Grace was doing so well that she may live into her teenage years! Good news! That was longer than her first prognosis, but it still seemed too short. Then again, she really had no idea. The doctors had the information and statistics and their educated guesses, but only God really knew the number of days Grace had.

In my Bible study at that time, we were learning about the leper who had been healed by Jesus. In Luke 5:12 the leper saw Jesus, then fell on his face and implored Him, saying, "Lord, if you are willing, you can make me clean." He came so humbly to Jesus, wanting only what Jesus thought was best. How convicted I was to seek God humbly in regard to Grace's life, as the leper did, and for God's will to be done in her life. I so often asked according to my own desires. I didn't want to go through the pain of losing her, nor did I want my family to go through that. But I needed to seek God's eternal purpose for Grace's life. I struggled with the need to make sure Grace's life had eternal purpose that I could see. I thought that if I was not faithful to proclaim God's goodness and His miracles that He might choose to take her home to heaven sooner. I just did not know how to let go of these struggles. No matter how many times I handed them over to God, they still seemed to come back around. When would I finally have the lasting resolve that God's purpose and plan for Grace's life would indeed be complete regardless of what I did or didn't do? Her life span was not dependent on me!

Grace's second birthday came around that year, and although it was a small celebration in numbers, it was a huge celebration in my heart! She had made it over so many hurdles that year and was such a strong fighter. She was such a treasure in our family. Grace adored her big brothers and sister. She would smile and respond to them immediately when they came near. They adored her also. I was so thankful that they wanted to be involved in her life and wanted her to be in their lives. There was no embarrassment, no shame, just pure pride whenever Grace was at their school for events or church. They knew she was a miracle!

On April 21, we had an appointment with yet another neurosurgeon—a much friendlier and more personable one! This is the one we would choose to do the tethered spinal cord surgery. God was so good to provide someone we could trust.

April 28 was our follow-up appointment with the cardiologist. He was so very excited about how well the balloon procedure was holding her aorta! Her mitral valve looked and sounded better. Her arm blood pressures had gone way down. He asked for any differences that I had noticed since her procedure. I told him her legs were definitely stronger and her energy level was better. She also had started to sleep for longer timeframes, up to six or seven hours at a time. This was really new! Now, if she could just figure out that nighttime is from 11:00 p.m. to 6:00 a.m., it would be really great. She was thinking bedtime was from 7:30 p.m. to 3:30 a.m., not quite matching up with my schedule. We could work with it, though! He would not have to put her on any high blood pressure medicine at this time. This was a big prize considering how much medication Grace was on for other things. He was still apologizing for not finding the murmur sooner but was just so excited and happy. I don't think I truly had realized how important and great this procedure was for Grace until I saw his excitement that day! I did not want to be so focused on all the distractions that I missed being grateful for what God was obviously doing to help our little girl.

There was so much to be grateful for. Our family was together. Rich had a great job that God provided. We had a beautiful home in northern San Antonio and loved the people, the weather, and many things about San Antonio. We were incredibly grateful for a wonderful Christian school where the staff and families loved my kids and loved our family. They were very quick to be helpful when it was needed. They were very faithful to pray for us. The same was true for our church. They were very friendly and helpful. We were getting quite attached to the church secretary and she was getting attached to us as well, especially to Gracie. She had offered to keep Grace in her office during Sunday school and to do Sunday school with just her and Grace so that Rich and I would be able to go to our own class. One of the very first Sundays in class I had the opportunity to share about Grace and the miracle that she was. After class I was surprised that a gentleman from class followed me all the way to the other building where Grace was with Miss Bonnie. He immediately knelt down beside Grace in her kid-kart, held her hand, and prayed for her. I had never seen anyone do that before. For him to obediently listen to God's call and humbly come seeking out my little girl to pray for her was such a blessing to me and to Grace. I desire to be that quick to obey God's call when He speaks to me ever so softly.

God had also very carefully placed us with each doctor and specialist. Grace's pediatrician lost the ability to accept Medicaid when one of her partners left. We had good insurance, but Medicaid covered everything else that insurance wouldn't. This was still crucial for our family as Grace's medical bills were many and they were large. This wonderful pediatrician did not want to send us on to another doctor, so she worked it out for us to stay and we did not have to pay the fees that had formerly been covered by Medicaid. I knew that was a sacrifice for her and we greatly appreciated it! She had obviously grown to love Grace as well as my other children. Yes, God had definitely provided for our family in this move, just as I knew He would. His faithfulness and His provision were very good.

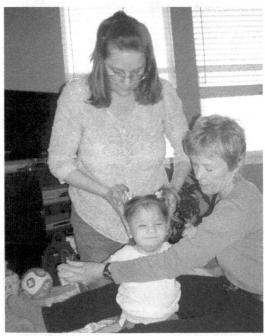

Physical Therapist and Occupational Therapist

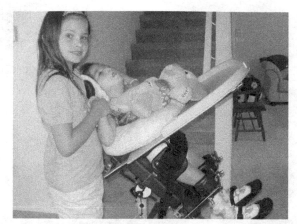

Grace in the stander with Megan close by

Sleepsafe Bed

Cami and Grace

5

Strong Enough

Proverbs 18:10, "The name of the Lord is a strong tower; the righteous run to it and are safe."

Strong enough . . . was I strong enough on my own? Could I be strong enough on my own? Did I want to be strong enough? Every time the song "Strong Enough" by Matthew West came on the radio, it seemed like it was meant just for me. In fact, I had people tell me that they thought of me when they heard this song! I also had people tell me from the time we received the news during the pregnancy throughout the next years, "Oh, you must be really strong" or "God must think you are really strong." Was I truly that strong? Did God really view me as strong? Or did He just know me so well because He had made me and He knew how I would respond? Maybe He saw me as someone who was willing to be molded, refined, strengthened. I hoped that was how He saw me. All I know is that I felt like it was a blessing that I was chosen to be Grace's mom. I had always felt like being a mom was a special calling. I knew that God had purposefully chosen which children would need me as their mom and that He blessed me with each uniquely made child He had given me. I shared that at a baby shower where I had the privilege of speaking a few years ago. I treasured Grace as I did my other three children. As much as I wanted to treat her and love her the same as I did my other children, there was a different thought process that was involved with Grace. I loved sharing my children with others to be enjoyed and loved, but with Grace, I felt like it was my job to bring God glory as much as possible through her life. I was not to keep this miracle to myself. Yes, all of my children were miracles—I believe each new life is a miracle and a gift from God—but my time with this little one was going to be cut short. God had told me through that song from early on to praise Him through it all. So if God chose me to be Grace's mom, and He called me to praise Him through her life, I knew that He would give me the strength to do it.

"Strong Enough" was a reminder to me that when I was weak or if it seemed like more than I could do, God would be strong enough for the both of us.

By May 2009, most people might think that the emotional side of this roller coaster ride would be under control. After all, we had celebrated Grace's second birthday in April! Yes, we had settled into life in San Antonio with new doctors, specialists, nurses in our home, therapists, hospitals, and an entire new support system of friends in the new church as well as the school. Somewhere along the way, I had read that when you have a medically fragile child, you continue going through the grieving stages in your own life. Not only do you grieve the death of many of your hopes and dreams for that child, but you grieve her death even though it may not be imminent. I cannot say that this was necessarily true for everyone in our family, although they had their concerns and worries. It definitely proved to be true for me. I do not feel like I grieved my hopes and dreams for Grace, because we received her diagnosis so early that my hopes and dreams became a much different list. Instead of dreaming of Grace doing well in school, playing sports, dating, getting married, and having her own family, I just hoped that she would be healthy and happy. I hoped that she would always know how much she was loved by us and by God. I hoped that she would be able to enjoy life in as many ways as we could possibly help her to.

The grieving that I periodically went through was entirely about the thought of losing Grace, her death, and how difficult that would be, not just for me, but for our whole family. It was a silent grieving, one that I did alone. I tried desperately to hide it from my kids, from Rich, other family members, and even my closest friends. I did not want to cause extra worry on their part for Grace or for me. I also didn't think that anyone would truly understand or that anyone could relate to me. After all, I did not see the same sadness or certainty of loss in anyone else. From the outside looking in, most just saw us as a happy family loving each other. In our home there was much joy, games like hide-and-seek, singing and dancing, cuddle time, and all the other wonderful times had with four children in the home! My times of grieving were done in private in my home when the kids were gone to school or busy playing with each other, on my runs, or in my van. They would come after difficult doctor's appointments, during hospitalizations, even on ordinary days when I least expected to feel the grief. I was not entirely alone though. In my grief I always knew that Jesus was right there with me. There would be a heavy heart and then the release of tears, crying out to my Lord and Savior who had brought me this far and I knew would continue to carry me through what was to come.

Deuteronomy 31:6, "Be strong and courageous. Do not be afraid or terrified because of them, for the Lord your God goes with you; he will never leave you nor forsake you."

On May 19, I journaled, "Okay, Lord," which usually meant that I was not very enthused with life and what was on my mind. Normally, I am so thankful that God is choosing to work in me that I don't mind the circumstances so much. This time was different though. I had gone through times of grieving before and after Grace's birth, but this time it seemed to be lasting for a long time. Many times the Lord would speak so clearly to me through music on the Christian radio station, and this was again one of those times. My time of grieving and sadness began when one song after another seemed to be directed straight to my heart and they all seemed to be pointing to Grace's death. Many were songs that I had learned to praise God through, actually looking forward to Grace's and my own homegoing! I knew heaven was not a place to be feared. Most of the time I just rejoiced in the thought of heaven, even realizing that we would most likely not enter heaven at the same time. Songs like "Praise You In This Storm," "There will be a Day," "Always," and "Held" were some of my favorites. And yet at this time, they were bringing me great sadness and feelings of complete brokenness. I didn't share these thoughts and feelings with anyone simply because I did not want to be the person who always had drama in her life. I didn't want to be the person everyone felt sorry for. *No one should feel sorry for me,* I thought, *for I had been blessed beyond measure.* Each day with Grace was more than I could have ever imagined I would get, and yet I yearned for the security of knowing there would be many more.

So, why all the sadness? What was God trying to teach me through this? On this particular day when I went on my run, nothing felt good: my legs were tight, my body ached, and I was not physically or mentally strong. I had been feeling led to do a half-marathon, possibly in November. Then I started wondering, *Why would God put that thought in my heart and head?* I had never had a "bucket list" or thought that I had to do that by a certain age. That just wasn't me! Could it be because Grace would not be here and I would need to focus and work toward something new? Why was I always trying to figure out God's motivation and plan? Why could I not just rest in Him and His plan?

As I started running up the hill, I was reminded that "when I am weak, then I am strong" (2 Cor. 12:10). As I thought of losing Grace on that run, He showed me that He would continue to give me every breath and footstep I would need to keep going. It would not be in my strength to do that, but I would need to keep going, keep living for the sake of Rich and my other three children. And when the time came that I felt I absolutely could not take another step, and yes, I was wanting to quit on my run, that He would carry me. Just as I felt each block was in its own way difficult to make it through that day, I knew that God would help me make it, day by day, hour by hour, and minute by minute. I could and would cry out to Him for the strength to make it through each moment when I felt I could not carry on or keep going. I knew at that time that this was a lesson the Lord really wanted me to learn. It seemed that He kept putting it right in my face. It was all the things that I had a knowledge of for such a long time, but this day, May 19, 2009, it seemed so incredibly personal.

From my journal: "Lord, I will learn this lesson even though it's a lesson I do not want to have to learn. I don't want to learn it ever, especially today, not now. Because if I learn this lesson, then that makes Grace's death that much closer to us. Lord, my heart aches at the thought, but I will do my best to learn this lesson, to remember what you have been showing me and teaching me. So for today I say, 'Okay, Lord.'"

The next day the heaviness had lifted some and I was feeling like I had some victory in that area. Yes, the loss of Grace still weighed on my thoughts, but not as heavily. Then the very next day I was struggling through my run again! I didn't understand why I physically felt so weak. I ran every day! As I struggled along, I was analyzing why I was so weak. *What had my diet been like lately? Had I been stretching? Was I getting enough rest? Would there be a better time of day to run according to when I ate my meals and when the heat would not be so bad?* As I was thinking through how to strengthen my body to be more ready for a run, God laid it on my heart that I needed to strengthen my soul and my spirit for whatever was coming. I naturally assumed it had something to do with Grace. He also laid it on my heart to intentionally use the coming summer months to strengthen my children for what was coming. God did not let me know when it was coming and, to be honest, He didn't even make it clear that it was about Grace.

My mother's health had not been good lately and I was very unsure about her tomorrows. I had no way of knowing what God's plan was, but I did know that if Grace's kidneys started failing, we would see it coming and it could be very slow and difficult to watch. Either way, whatever God was doing, we needed to be strengthened. I was certain of that.

Now the question was, how to do that? I had already felt the need to have our summer be less busy. There would be some family visiting and the boys would go to Bible camp. Megan and Ethan would do a couple of camps at their school all in the same week. They would also play some baseball for the YMCA. There would be Grace's surgery and possibly a trip up north to see family. This schedule for summer seemed light, believe it or not. I would definitely plan on doing devotions with the kids regularly and trying to be more open in giving the kids time to talk about what God was showing them. I definitely needed to make time for myself to be in God's Word, praying and soaking in all that He needed to teach me. I needed to be ready for whatever was coming.

Then God also laid it on my heart to be praying about *everything* this summer. I had no idea how I would be when we lost Grace or if my kids would want to talk to me about it, but I knew if I could teach them to run to God for everything, that would be the best thing I could ever do for them.

My journal: "Lord, please help me to be intentional with my children this summer. Please help me to not get distracted and lose my focus."

School finished at the end of May and summer was in full swing with ball practices and games, swimming, keeping the kids entertained at home, and family coming to visit! My sister came for her visit in June just as planned. Grace had been cleared for her surgery, but then started running a fever the same day it was scheduled to be done. She ended up in the ER as well as the hospital for three days, but no surgery was done on her spinal cord. She had C-Diff (Clostridiumdifficile), which meant she was having diarrhea and throwing up, caused by being on antibiotics too much, mostly from treating the UTIs. The antibiotics killed the good bacteria in Grace's stomach and she was unable to fight the other illnesses. It seemed so confusing that the very antibiotics that we used to heal her from one issue could also cause her great sickness. My sweet little girl was very sick. Her bi-carb count was 15 when it was supposed to be 23. Her glucose count was 19 when it was supposed to be 60 or greater. She was also very dehydrated from the prolonged diarrhea. Thankfully they knew exactly what needed to be done for her. The surgery was postponed to July 22, when hopefully she would be well. We were able to really enjoy our time with my sister once Grace was released from the hospital. Then our next guests were my brother and his family! It was really special to be able to enjoy the area where we lived with family.

We also had Vacation Bible School in June. The big highlight for me was singing with Grace and the 200+ kids at Bible school. The wilder and crazier the kids and adults were, the bigger Gracie's grin. She loved it and you could see it all over her face! We had been in the habit with Gracie of raising her arms up in the air and saying, "Praise Jesus!" Or if she raised her arms up, we would say "Praise Jesus!" At one point in the song "Get Down" by Audio Adrenaline, Gracie raised both arms up into the sky as if she herself were praising Jesus! I truly think she was, but if not, she sure had the joy of the Lord in that moment! What a blessing for me to see! I absolutely loved our church. They had been such a blessing to our family. They cared about us and prayed for us. Everything they did was done with excellence and love. Eric, Ethan, and Megan were all wanting to be baptized! They seem to be growing and understanding their faith and God's Word more each day.

On Monday, June 29, the kids and I planned to travel north to visit family and friends up in the Midwest. Of course, the weekend before we were to leave, Grace started gagging and having some diarrhea again. We questioned whether or not we should go, but with a lot of prayers and a lot of Pedialyte, we ventured off. God was good and cleared up the diarrhea in the next few days. Grace still ran a fever once in a while, but we were able to complete our trip and see many friends and family from Nebraska, Iowa, South Dakota, and Minnesota. We really made the most of our time and in return we were so blessed and encouraged. I had started a CaringBridge website page for Grace shortly after moving to San Antonio. I had seen how well it worked for a friend in their time of medical crisis and couldn't think of a better way to share news about our family, especially Grace and her praises, as well as prayer requests concerning her.

As soon as we returned to Texas, our schedule was filled up with Grace's many doctor's appointments, therapy sessions, and blood-work. As we were waiting in the doctor's office one day, Grace and I were doing our usual stuff to enjoy our time while waiting. I would lotion her, comb her hair, play with toys, read books, or sing songs. She and I always enjoyed our many moments waiting together. At this particular appointment, I was holding Grace's hand and I was remind-ing her that Mommy would always try to be there to hold her hand through the many hard things she had to go through: the urine cul-tures, needle pokes for bloodwork, x-rays, IVs, and the many doctors' checks. While I was doing this, the visual thought came to my mind of me holding Grace's hand until the day I would give that sweet little hand to Jesus. When that day came, she would not need my hand any more to get through the aches and pains of her medically fragile life or to help her not be afraid. Instead she would have the hand of her Savior, who had never left her alone. As hard as I tried or as much as my heart desired to always be there for Grace, there were times when someone else had to be there with her: the nurse at our home while I went on field trips with my other kids or simply to the store, a couple nights a week when I slept and entrusted her to a night nurse, or I just entrusted her to Jesus to watch over her, knowing that I had to sleep. When Grace got to heaven, she would never be alone.

***

Rich and I had been talking about the fact that his job at this hotel was getting more stressful. Also, the hotel was so far from our home that much of his day was wasted driving to and from work. With the crazy traffic at rush hour, he would leave early and come home really late just to avoid it. He was starting to see the need to be looking for another job, which usually meant another move to yet another city. We had only been in San Antonio for a little over a year and loved it there. My stomach felt sick as Rich told me about the different cities where hotels were possibly available. He was excited about a new opportunity, but all I could see were the many hurdles ahead.

A move would mean a totally new health care system for Grace: new hospitals, ERs, doctors, therapists, a new Medicaid plan (if they had one), and did I mention the many doctors? Then there was also the major task of getting the house ready to sell, the multiple times of cleaning it for showings and the ongoing attempt to keep it as perfect as possible while living in it! Also, there was the tough job of being a single mom for who knows how long since Rich always had to go ahead of the family and we always had to wait for the house to sell. This could be a short time or it could be a very long time and we had just done it! Then there was always the task of finding a new church and school and house. Along with another relocation came the loss of friends, and the need for new ones. Not just friends you go have coffee with once in a great while, but friends you can call on in an emergency, because those emergency situations would definitely happen. Only God knew how quickly they would come, how many, and how often. My kids also would need new friends and it's always so hard making them start over again. It wasn't bad when they were little, but now that they were in school, it just was. I did want Rich to have a hotel closer to home. We were not seeing much of him. I wanted him to feel secure in his job and for it to be peaceful and one that he enjoyed. We had been praying that God would allow us to stay in Texas, but I honestly just wanted to be where God wanted us to be. In my heart, I knew that God would help us through and He could help us love a new home and city even more than we loved San Antonio. His plan for us would surely be good!

With all of these moving possibilities fresh in my mind, the next day I went on my run and God brought to my mind two different songs.

Petra had a song, "I Will Call Upon The Lord," written by Michael O'Shields: "I will call upon the Lord, who is worthy to be praised. So shall I be saved from my enemies, I will call upon the Lord."

God was in the process of saving us from the enemy. I felt like the people at that job in San Antonio did not have Rich's best interest at heart, and God was taking us away from there because the enemy was using that against us. I praised the Lord that He was showing me that!

The next song that came to me was "He Is Able" written by Henry Smith, "He is able, more than able, to accomplish what concerns me today. He is able, more than able, to handle anything that comes my way. He is able, more than able, to do much more than I could ever dream. He is able, more than able, to make me what He wants me to be."

Once again, God was so good at reassuring me right when I needed it most. Yes, I felt very incapable of moving again, and I just honestly didn't want to, but I knew God was able to handle every part of whatever move or change He had planned for us and I would choose to trust Him.

Grace's surgery was never accomplished that summer. We tried scheduling it four different times, once in June, then July 22, July 29, and finally August 12. Each time, Grace was sick. First it was C-Diff, then ear infections, then a UTI, and then a bacterial infection. Through those summer months we were constantly in and out of the doctor's office and the ER. Grace ran fevers continuously. We would just get on an antibiotic for one infection and then another infection would creep in. She even had thrush, which is a yeast infection in the mouth that comes from antibiotics and inhalers. Once again, the very things we were trying to keep her healthy with were making her sick. I did not understand why God kept stopping the plan. I did know many people including myself had been praying for God to be clear on this surgery, to make her healthy for it, and to protect her through it. So after four times I knew that God did not want Grace's surgery to be done at this time in her life. I was very upset about the clear "no" He was giving each time. The only reason I could think of was that Grace's numbered days were perhaps not as long as my desire and that God did not see fit to put Grace through that suffering if it was not going to extend her life anyway. That was hard for me to think about. It gave me a very heavy heart once again. I did eventually have peace that we were not to re-schedule yet again. A doctor from our church suggested possibly scheduling for Christmas break or spring; maybe God would have revealed His reason by then. That sounded very wise to me. So for now, we would just try to keep her as healthy as could be and enjoy all of these wonderful days that we were being blessed with while she was here! God also continued to give Scripture to give me peace as well.

Isaiah 26:3, "You will keep in perfect peace him whose mind is steadfast, because he trusts in you."

Acts 17:25, "He himself gives all men life and breath and everything else."

God knew Grace's needs and her body. I was trusting that He would satisfy every need that she had concerning her kidneys and bladder and all else.

***

Throughout the summer we continued to struggle through our nights. I was thankful when we started getting a night nurse to come two nights a week. After that, for those two nights, I was able to shut our bedroom door and shut off the monitor, most of the time. Grace's typical day would be a thirty-minute nap in the morning. Then she would fall asleep mid-afternoon and sleep soundly until late evening (from approximately 2:30–9:30 p.m.). Then Grace would sleep two to three hours in the night. The rest of the night, Grace would be wide awake kicking, smiling, and talking rather loudly. I am sure that she thought it was play time since she was in the same bedroom with big sister, Megan! I don't know how Megan managed to sleep through it all, but she usually did. I would have been tempted to change the sleeping arrangements, but Megan insisted that she wanted to share rooms with Grace.

We tried everything to keep Grace awake during the day. We took her shopping, did bath time, therapy sessions, put her in the middle of three loud siblings, and even swimming. She would maybe wake up for a few moments, but never for long. I remember her therapists just laughing because Grace slept through all of the stretching and other activities they would try to do with her. God was indeed gracious to give me the strength to keep on going. We did eventually make some progress in this area in the summer as we would let Grace sleep two hours and then take her swimming with us. She loved swimming so much that she would wake up for a while. Then it was just the challenge of keeping her awake through the evening. We worked at it this way for a while, and then decided to try shifting Grace's schedule by a couple hours a day until we eventually got it to where we wanted it. But Grace was not cooperating very well. We managed to move her bedtime up to 9:45 in the morning, then two days later after taking two half-hour naps in the night I was able to get her to go to bed by 6:45 a.m. This was really sad when 6:45 a.m. bedtime was thought of as progress, but we were just trying to persevere through the plan. A couple nights later I managed to get her to bed by 4:00 a.m. Then the next night she fell asleep at 2:30 a.m. The next night we went to a resort for a short trip before school started. Thankfully, Grace went to sleep at 1:30 a.m. By August 27, 2009, Grace slept from midnight to 7:00 a.m. That was exciting news for this momma!

Grace had been running a fever off and on all week. When we took her in to the doctor this time, her urine and ears looked good. The doctor thought that Grace's fevers were due to her brain stem not regulating her temperature. I knew this was true, but Grace tended to run too cold, not too hot. It was frustrating that we did not really have an answer for the fevers. Plus, if that was indeed true, then how and when would I know when it was just her brain stem not working correctly? How would I know when it was a fever that needed attention, perhaps another UTI or ear infection?

By September 2009, Grace was doing fairly well. We were back to having our same sleep schedule struggles and the fevers were still on and off with no answers as to their cause, but I felt like she was good overall! It was also in September that God answered our prayers about Rich's job situation. He was offered a job at a hotel in Albuquerque, New Mexico. He had considered a couple others before that, but none of them seemed right. We'd lived in Albuquerque some years ago for a short six months, but God had made it a good six months. He really had put it in our hearts as a wonderful place with good memories and kind people. It seemed perfect. We were all a bit sad to be leaving San Antonio because we all loved it there, but we knew that God was working in the circumstances of our lives and guiding us to where we would go. So we put our home on the market and trusted God to make the path smooth.

Isaiah 45:2, "I will go before you and will level the mountains."

Rich would leave in the next week for New Mexico, but not until we had all witnessed Eric, Ethan, and Megan being baptized at our church in San Antonio. We were also very grateful that Rich's father was able to fly down for the weekend to be with us for the baptism. How special it was to have him there!

One thing I had learned through my pregnancy was that I needed to be studying God's Word and I needed to be having fellowship with Christian ladies. At our church there were definitely wonderful godly women available, but the Bible studies available were not very easy for me to get to with Grace. So I decided to offer a Bible study at my house! I talked with another gal who said she would help lead it and we started doing some Beth Moore Bible studies at our house. I remember one day specifically in our study that we were talking about the difference between going through a valley and being on the mountaintop. The valley tended to always be portrayed as the struggle, the difficult times in our lives. The mountaintop was always portrayed as those awesome moments in our lives where we felt so close to God, perhaps at a Bible camp or retreat where you felt you had maybe heard from God or He had felt so close. On the mountaintop you would come away with such an excited happy feeling that you were growing closer to God in your faith. The valley was just the rough moment that you couldn't wait to get through and be done with. It was those moments in life that you didn't choose, yet had to go through. So the mountaintop experiences were the moments or times you desired to have more of!

That day I did not have a nurse. It was an opportunity for me to love on Grace more, so I was standing with Gracie in my arms rocking her back and forth, listening to the conversation unfold about everyone's mountaintop experiences. Had I had some mountaintop experiences? Yes, many times at Bible camps, Bible college, and other times. But the thought that struck me the most that I had to share with the ladies that day was that my biggest "mountaintop" experience when I felt closest to my Lord, when I knew I was growing in my faith, when I knew I was hearing from God often, was not at some amazing retreat listening to a great speaker in the middle of a camp in the beautiful mountains, but rather it was truly in my valley. My "valley," technically, had been going on for over two years. Not to say that my pregnancy with Gracie, her birth, and her life were a valley of despair and hardship. It was a valley of constant leaning on the Lord for strength and hope. Yes, Grace brought much joy to our home. We praised God for her each day! But it was also such a time of uncertainty which could turn to anxiety, stress, loneliness, and depression at a moment's notice. It was a challenge that came when my body was at its worst physical time as well, constantly being so tired from lack of sleep. I lived on Mountain Dew! There was also the constant guilt of not being able to be everything for everyone. Grace required more attention. A child who is medically fragile just does and that's a fact. Fighting the constant guilt of not being a good enough wife, or not feeling like I was giving my other three children enough attention, time, and love was a battle I always fought in my heart. In my mind, I was in a valley, fighting a battle every day. Yet, I was also having many mountaintop experiences. I was seeing God do miracles and answer prayers! I was hearing from God, not audibly, but through songs, His Word, and the Holy Spirit. I was praying and doing Bible study diligently.

In San Antonio, I was at the beginning of many new friendships that were good, but I did not have any deep, close friendships that had stood the test of time like I'd had in Omaha. Rich was gone early morning until late at night with work most days, and to be honest, our relationship was not as close as it should have been. Jesus became that friend for me. He was the only One who truly knew my heart, my feelings, my hurts, my pains, and my joys. He was the only One who was there for me and with me through every second of every day, good or bad. I shared with the ladies that day that I didn't want my valley/mountaintop experiences to end, because that would mean that Grace would not be with us anymore. I knew that would mean heaven for Grace, which would be amazing for her and complete healing for her! But I wasn't sure what life without Grace looked like for me, and I didn't want to find out.

Yes, God had made me strong enough for what I was going through in every moment of those days with Grace in our lives. The things I was doing for Grace medically were things most people get major schooling and training for. I usually had to learn them in a thirty-second training session from a nurse or doctor. God continued to build up in me the emotional strength that I needed. He gave me the physical strength to lift her along with her very heavy kid-cart/wheelchair and other medical equipment. He gave me the physical strength to keep taking care of my family on very little sleep for such a long time. Would He make me strong enough for life without her?

***

Grace had been put on a cancellation list for her spinal surgery toward the end of September. If the doctor received a cancellation, they would call us. If Grace was healthy, we would get it done. This seemed like a good plan to me. I still felt that she needed the surgery, but I didn't have to be the one to work so hard to make her healthy. If God wanted her to have the surgery, it would be on His perfect timing and plan. Sure enough, by October 9, the doctor's office had called and wanted to do the surgery. Rich was in Albuquerque with no way to be home for the surgery or the hospital time it involved. I was very thankful for the kids' friends and their families at the school who offered to take each of my kids in once again. I know Eric, Ethan, and Megan were nervous and scared for their sister, but they were able to enjoy being with friends. They each went to a different home for about a week as Grace had her surgery and hospital time. I was also very blessed by some wonderful ladies and the pastor and his wife coming to the hospital to sit with me while Grace had her surgery. There were people from church who came to visit us in the hospital and a friend who came to sit with Grace for a few hours while I went and had lunch with my other children at school. There were people who worked out my transportation problems by letting me drive their BIG truck while they fixed my vehicle. There were others who brought meals to the house once we got home, and a friend who stayed with Grace once I got her home so I could go pick up Eric, Ethan, and Megan. I was not left alone even with Rich out of town. God provided for every need we had. I know I was not strong enough to handle everything, but I knew that God would take care of every detail and that He was strong enough. When a person knows that, then they are strong.

The surgery was very successful. The filum (part of spine that they cut) was so taut, it bounced right up when it was cut. This led the surgeon to believe there must have been a great deal of pressure there. The surgery was shorter than expected and it was tough to wake Grace up, but the second I walked in the room and she heard my voice she was awake. She stayed awake long enough to hear her daddy's voice on the phone. She had that sweet look on her face that was so close to a smile, but she was obviously too tired to fully smile. Then she dozed back off to sleep.

Grace ran a fever for almost two weeks after surgery. She had another UTI. I knew the surgery was not a guarantee for no more UTI's and only time would tell. I was always amazed that Grace would have a fever with her UTI for days even after the antibiotic was given. Then usually the day after I asked for prayer on her CaringBridge website, the fever would disappear.

By the end of October, some large items we had been hoping to get for Grace before we moved were approved and ordered. One was a stander, which is a heavy-duty piece of equipment that we would lay Grace in horizontally, strap her legs and body in, and then transition her from horizontal to whatever degree of vertical Grace was ready for. The stander was to build the muscle up in her legs so she would be able to stand on her own in the process of getting ready to walk. We did this twice a day for a half-hour each time. We also received a SleepSafe Bed. This was a specially made bed with high padded sides that would work well for her as she continued to grow. These would both be greatly beneficial to Grace's care! These were very expensive pieces of equipment that the wonderful state of Texas paid for! We were again grateful for answered prayers.

Grace continued running fevers throughout October and into November. By early November we saw a surgeon about the continuing issues with Grace's feeding tube. The hole had become too large and was constantly draining, which was causing major skin issues on her stomach. Her skin was just red and raw. The doctor also had some concerns about the stoma, the opening into her abdomen surrounding it. He decided that her stomach was in a critical state and that she needed surgery to put a feeding tube into her stomach. This would give the skin on her stomach the ability to heal, as well as give Grace some freedom in the future as she would not be tied to a feeding tube and bag all the time. She was starting to roll and move more, so that would be great! It would be a simple surgery and was expected to be fairly easy to recover from and deal with at home afterwards. The surgery was scheduled for December 4, and we had everyone praying for Grace to be healthy enough to get it done.

On Monday morning, November 30, I drove the boys to school as usual, but I brought Megan home as she was sick. I called to make Megan a doctor's appointment. I didn't want to take Grace to the appointment and expose her to more illnesses, so I called our nursing agency to see if our normal day nurse (who came two days a week) could come in for part of the day. They called back quickly to say that she could and would arrive at 10:30 a.m. Soon after I made that call, Grace started having some bad seizures, and I helped her through them while Megan lay on the couch. When Grace started gagging and passing a lot of gas, I quickly shut off her feeds, thinking, *Grace must have a stomach virus.*

Megan was sick with a cough and fever. Grace had a fever also. Grace seemed to calm down and was going to sleep on the loveseat, so I turned my attention back to Megan. My nurse arrived on time and started her assessment of Grace. She noticed right away that Grace's little heart was racing and that she was hardly breathing. At that point, I looked closely at Grace and realized that she was not sleeping as I thought, but rather was in a lethargic state and was getting blue around her lips. The nurse and I immediately got the oxygen tank out of the closet and put Grace on oxygen. That seemed to slow her heart rate down quickly, but her breathing was still shallow and she just didn't seem to want to breathe. I called the doctor to see where we should take her and she told us to call 911. That is what we did.

The ambulance came quickly and Grace's oxygen level immediately went up in the ambulance. Grace finally started to turn her head in response again. The fear in my heart finally had a little comfort and reassurance that Grace would be alright. At the hospital they ran the normal tests. Grace had strep pneumonia, a UTI, and a virus that may or may not be related to the pneumonia. They took very good care of her. We almost had to stay the night, but since we had oxygen available at home and a nurse that night and the next day, they allowed me to take her home. I was relieved that I could go home and take care of Grace and Megan and the boys. The next couple of days would be critical for Grace and once again her surgery was postponed.

By the next day, Megan was worse and Grace was still in rough shape. When we went to the doctor's office, the doctor sent me with both girls to the ER where they were both then admitted to the hospital—talk about life in chaos! Rich was in New Mexico, my boys were at school expecting me to pick them up at the end of the day, and now I was getting my girls admitted to the hospital! In the ER Megan and Grace were in separate rooms, and I kept going back and forth. Thankfully the girls were able to share a room once they were admitted to the hospital. Grace was treated with IV antibiotics for her strep pneumonia, virus, and UTI. Megan, who was actually sicker than Grace on that day, was given breathing treatments and IV antibiotics for her pneumonia, which was not the same pneumonia that her sister had! Two days later I was able to bring both girls home. We continued breathing treatments for both girls for a few more days, but at least we were all able to rest better at home. Megan especially did not like her hospital stay. She absolutely hated the IV, the breathing treatments, pretty much every part of her hospital stay. The only part she liked was that she was with her baby sister! I could only hope that both girls would heal quickly.

While both girls appeared to recover from their pneumonia and breathing difficulties, it was not long before Grace was awake most of each night crying in pain. I was fortunate to have a night nurse and she tried her best to soothe Grace, but I could hear everything. When your baby girl is doubled over in pain, you do everything you can to try to help her. It had to be a stomach virus. I had taken her to the ER a couple days before and they found nothing. On the way to the hospital on Monday, I realized that the van ride calmed her down. So the next day, after Grace had cried for three hours, I put her in the van and went driving. It calmed her down. The next night she slept from 2:00 to 4:00 a.m. She woke crying in pain again and we headed straight for the van. Carefully driving through the streets of northern San Antonio in the dead of night, Grace calmed down. Grace's seizure activity had also increased during this illness, and, once again, I got on her CaringBridge site and asked for prayers.

Grace's surgery for her stomach had been pushed back to December 18. That would be the last day she'd be on her present antibiotic and would be her best chance of being healthy. The plan was to do a Fundo, which is when they wrap up the bottom of the esophagus and the top of the stomach to prevent refluxing and aspirating, and then put in a G-button. This would put the formula right into her stomach. She would also not be attached to the feeding bag and tube all the time. This was critical to allow the skin on Grace's stomach time to heal. Her GJ tube site, which had been done two years before, had become too big and leaked all the time. When she was sick, the leak would be worse. The leaking stomach fluid was very acidic. It leaked all over her raw skin and was very painful. We tried desperately to keep it clean and dry, but this was really next to impossible. We were constantly putting ointment on it and protective barrier powder and changing the gauze. There was just no way to make it better. We were just trying to manage the pain.

Grace's surgery went well, but she immediately had difficulties afterwards. They finished her surgery at about 4:00 p.m. By that evening, Grace was in pain. She was very congested and her oxygen level was between 89 and 93; a good oxygen level should be between 95 and 100. I suctioned her and her oxygen level went down to 88. Grace was very lethargic, limp, and non-responsive. I stopped suctioning to wait for her oxygen level to come up, and all of a sudden, it started plummeting down to 48! I pushed the nurse call button several times and no one was coming! I was very scared and ran to the hall, crying and calling out for a nurse. Someone came to my aid and got a nurse. They quickly put Grace on oxygen and Grace's level immediately came up to 98. We left the oxygen on for several minutes and then tried to take it off. Again her level dropped to 78, so the oxygen was put back on. The nurses called the doctor to come and assess her to decide if Grace needed to be moved to the PICU. They did a lung x-ray and checked her blood. Her blood sugar level was too low to read—a 6. They gave her a bolus of glucose and fifteen minutes later Grace was kicking and swinging her arms around. What a difference!

I couldn't help but feel responsible. I had shut off her feeds at 10:00 p.m. the night before and for some time during the day before to try to give her tummy time to heal. It was the only way to stop the draining. I honestly didn't know what would have been the right thing to do but was thankful that Grace did well through the night with the oxygen on and her blood sugar level staying good.

By December 20, Grace had a high fever, her heart was racing, and she was still very congested. I told the nurse that the last time her heart raced like that, Grace had pneumonia. They called our pulmonary doctor and he ordered an x-ray. Sure enough, Grace had pneumonia. She was still not passing gas or having a bowel movement. The doctors would not start feeding her until she had one. Her heart had been racing and her oxygen levels were not the best. In an x-ray on December 22, they said that she had pneumonia again. Then two days later she tested positive for RSV, respiratory syncytial virus. Grace's fever that day was up to 102.9°, and at a friend's home, Megan's was 102.3°. My friend took Megan to the doctor and we found that she also had RSV! Grace's doctors at the hospital had told us how dangerous it would be for Megan to get RSV so soon after having pneumonia. Rich was in New Mexico and I had two very sick girls and I couldn't be with them both.

This was very hard with Christmas just a few days away. Thankfully, Megan started improving as soon as they put her on an antibiotic. But by Christmas Eve, Grace had become worse. She had RSV, pneumonia, and possibly a bacterial pneumonia as well. She was on 60 percent oxygen and the hospital decided to move Grace to the ICU. They were also concerned about Grace's heart, because they were having trouble finding her femoral artery. Grace's temperature had been up as high as 105.1° and was finally starting to come down as they put her on more oxygen and a Bi-PAP machine to support her breathing. Rich was finally on his way home late that evening.

Christmas day was to be a day filled with anticipation and joy and a special time with family. I was blessed by our pastor and his wife. They came to sit with Grace for a few hours so I could go home and spend that time with Rich and my three children. While I tried to put on a smile and pretend that everything was going to be alright, the truth was, I just didn't know. Grace's x-ray looked worse that morning. I tried to be hopeful, but inside I was filled with fear. Grace was so sick that I wasn't sure if she would make it through this time. As soon as I felt I had put in enough time at home to accomplish all of our Christmas musts, I drove quickly back to the hospital. The hospital blessed Grace with many gifts on Christmas day, including sheets, toys, and books. I had no idea that so many people gave to children's hospitals so the kids in the hospital would have a good Christmas as well!

Isaiah 41:10, "So do not fear, for I am with you; do not be dismayed, for I am your God. I will strengthen you and help you; I will uphold you with my righteous right hand."

***

The day after Christmas, Grace had to go on a ventilator. It would be a long slow process to get her off. The ventilator was a high-frequency ventilator that oscillates. It worked like a cool air humidifier sending in the air and also gently shaking Grace's little body non-stop, with the hope that it would loosen up the fluid in her lungs. The doctors checked Grace's blood gases around the clock and adjusted the ventilator accordingly. While the next x-ray did not look much better, Grace's temperatures were starting to gradually come down by December 29. Grace would need to move on to another ventilator in the next day or two and she'd have to be on that one for several days. This seemed like it would never end. Grace was handling her feeds well, but her body was retaining fluid and she started to look really swollen. Rich had to go back to New Mexico to work and the kids were back with friends. The longer they had to stay at other homes, the more they worried about Gracie. During this hospital stay, we would have a good day and then a bad day. It just seemed to go back and forth with the x-rays each day.

On December 30, Grace's x-ray looked worse and her blood gas levels were bad. Parts of Grace's lung, the upper right lobe, looked as if they were starting to collapse. It was a very discouraging day. Then the next day, the x-ray looked a little better. The truth was that Grace's lungs were still in a very critical state. The pneumonia was throughout both of her lungs; at the beginning it was just in the upper right and lower left. Grace was still a very sick little girl.

By December 31, Grace was on her sixth roommate. I was trying to pray for each child and family who joined us in our room and was thankful when each one would get better and get to go home, but as each family moved on with their lives, I wondered if it would ever be our turn. I tried to keep my eyes off myself and focus on the real reasons we were there. God's picture of our lives is always so much broader than what is right in front of our face. We have to keep our heads up, looking around, to see the many reasons He has placed us in the situations we are in. God had made me strong—strong for myself, strong for Grace, strong for Rich, strong for Eric, Ethan, and Megan, and even strong enough to still be able to encourage and pray for others around me. After all of our hospital stays, I believe this was the first one when I truly started seeing our hospital stays not just as a place where Grace could get better, but where my eyes could be opened to the many other families and children around me who were hurting and who needed prayers for hope, encouragement, and healing also.

1 Timothy 1:12, "I thank Christ Jesus our Lord, who has given me strength, that he considered me faithful, appointing me to his service."

The days turned into weeks as we waited for Grace to heal. We were thankful on January 3, 2010, when her fever finally came down. Her blood gases also were good enough to switch her over to the conventional ventilator and her temperature continued to come down. Rich had been home the previous weekend and slept at the hospital so I was finally able to go home and sleep in my own bed. The kids were also able to come home for the weekend. They were discouraged that they had hardly been home at all for Christmas break, and that they had to go back to their friends' houses again after the weekend. Our house had nearly sold on December 23, but we had to turn down the offer because the buyers wanted to move in by the first week of January. At the time of the offer, we weren't sure Grace would be alive by the end of the week. We weren't sure if we would be having a funeral or bringing her home from the hospital, and how could we do either if we had no home? The kids were also discouraged about that, because they just didn't understand why we would turn down the offer. We had to trust that God would sell the house again, and He would work everything out for our good.

My mom and friend Malinda made the trip down to San Antonio. They arrived on Wednesday, January 6, after a long drive. I was so grateful for the help, both at the hospital and at home. Eric, Ethan, and Megan were finally able to come home. By this time the doctors were talking about the need to get Grace off the ventilator. Her numbers still were not perfect, but the longer she was on it, the possibility of her getting more infections became more likely. That same Wednesday, they took Grace off the ventilator and she did really well. She was still on oxygen at a high percentage that was equal to what she had from the ventilator. The only difficult part was that Grace had become addicted to the sedation and pain medication while on the ventilator, and for the next week she would get upset even being touched. They put her back on some of the medications and decided to take her off slowly so her withdrawal symptoms would not be so severe.

January 12, 2010, was the wonderful day that Grace was finally released from the hospital and able to come home! We celebrated Grace's Christmas that night. The kids were ecstatic to have her home. If only Rich had been able to be there. The kids helped Grace open her gifts and played with them on her lap even though she was very sleepy through most of it. We celebrated with a special cake. Of course, the kids had no idea that Grace almost did not make it home from that hospital stay. I knew, though, and even though I was exhausted, it was one of the best celebrations ever.

Romans 5:3–4, "We also rejoice in our sufferings, because we know that suffering produces perseverance; perseverance, character; and character, hope. And hope does not disappoint us, because God has poured out his love into our hearts by the Holy Spirit, whom he has given us."

I hoped and prayed that God was producing perseverance, character, and hope in me as we went through this time of suffering. I always struggled with the question of why my little girl had to suffer so much so that I and others might grow. She was the one hurting, struggling to breathe, lying in the hospital bed for days and weeks, getting poked so many times for blood draws, IVs, and PICC lines that her poor little veins were getting harder to find each time, and all the while having the tube down her throat to get the necessary air into her lungs to be able to stay alive. It did not seem fair. *Why her, why not me?* I could allow these feelings to consume me if I wanted. I had to trust that God's ways were higher than mine as it tells us in Isaiah 55:8–9. I had to trust that, just as He was walking me through each step of this difficult journey, He was just as close to Grace, holding her hand, taking away her fear, and speaking words of encouragement and love into her very soul. He loved her. I knew that God, her Creator, loved her!

For the next several weeks, we would continue to wean Grace off the methadone she had been given for pain. She never got as irritable as she had been in the hospital, but as the weaning continued, her seizures continued to get worse. They were no longer the little startle seizures, but big seizures where Grace would hold her breath, with her arms stiff out to the side shaking, as well as her legs stiffening. We continued increasing the dosage of her seizure medications to try to get them under control. By February 17, she was averaging seven a day. By February 18, she was up to ten. We were told that sporadic seizures throughout the day were not as dangerous as they would be if they were often and close together. Five of these ten were within the same hour. Grace was still holding her breath through them, so we were always waiting for that next breath. I know many doctors say that you shouldn't do much of anything to a child when they are seizing, but ever since Grace was tiny, I had always picked her up and held her and loved on her whenever I was present for a seizure. I taught my nurses and everyone else around her to do the same, except Eric, Ethan, and Megan. Grace was getting heavy and I didn't think it was safe to have them trying to hold her through her seizures. They did however still cuddle on up to her in whatever chair she was in and hugged and loved her through her seizures. Each one of my kids loved her so much. I tried to stay calm through the seizures so they would not worry so much, but I know that on the inside, we all worried and we were all frightened.

Grace's seizures continued to increase. By February 21, she was averaging between ten and fourteen a day. Many of them were in the evening. I was grateful that they were later so the kids did not see many of them as they were in bed. On the rare occasion when I had a night nurse, we realized Grace was seizing during the night as well. This was especially frightening, because there was an initial very small sound Grace would make when the seizure began, but then she would hold her breath and there was nothing to hear, especially for a sleeping mother. One night I pinned a bell on the arm of Grace's pajamas, so when her arms flung out to the side I would hear the bell. Grace had slept for only three hours that night before I heard the bell. The rest of the night she was jingling quite regularly, but not just because of the seizures. She thought the bell was a fun addition to bedtime! I don't know how Megan slept through many of Grace's nights sharing the room. Either the nurse or I was in and out all night long.

By February 22, Grace was having fever on and off again and had had fifteen seizures. I took her in to get checked for a UTI or a sinus infection. As much as I did not want another UTI, I wanted an answer. *Surely the seizure activity increasing was due to an infection somewhere in her body?* We had no quick results, but the hospital put her on an antibiotic anyway. That same day, as I was holding Grace through her eighth seizure, I was singing a praise song. God brought to my mind the message on trials that our pastor had given the day before. Although I couldn't understand why Grace had to suffer for me to go through trials, I did know that God was strengthening me for that time. I also knew that the trials were meant to bring God glory. So I would continue to praise Him for the trials. He was in complete control. He created Grace and all of her medical challenges and He could choose to heal her of them in His perfect timing. He would sustain her and us through them. I would continue to pour out my heart to Him on her behalf for healing and trust in His perfect will. He blessed us with our precious little Gracie and I would give thanks!

> In this you greatly rejoice, though now for a little while you may have had to suffer grief in all kinds of trials. These have come so that your faith—of greater worth than gold, which perishes even though refined by fire—may be proved genuine and may result in praise, glory and honor when Jesus Christ is revealed. Though you have not seen him, you love him; and even though you do not see him now, you believe in him and are filled with an inexpressible and glorious joy, for you are receiving the goal of your faith, the salvation of your souls. (1 Peter 1:6–9)

Oh, how I desired for my faith to be of greater worth than gold, that it would be proved genuine and result in praise, glory, and honor to Christ. Was mine a perfect faith? Definitely not! I still had many doubts about His goodness and His plan. I still had fear of the future, which in truth is lack of trust. I would keep striving, though, not just through my years with Grace. It is something I will continue to strive after until the day that my faith becomes sight, when my salvation is complete, and I am in my heavenly home!

***

A few days later, we found out that Grace did have a UTI. They put her on a different antibiotic. Unfortunately, it did not slow down her seizures that were up to fifteen-plus a day. I was a bit more at peace about them, diligently keeping track of each seizure in a notebook. I thought that if I was documenting them, it may help us figure out how to slow them down. I was on a constant seizure watch; my eyes rarely ever left her little body. She was having small seizures as well as big ones.

Grace's seizures continued to progress. By the middle of March she was having forty-five to fifty seizures a day. Many were small, but some were bigger. I was working with the neurologist to see if her medications needed to be changed. Two of her medications were able to be increased. We thought that may be the answer, but she continued having fifty seizures a day. I had started taking her to a chiropractor to see if they would be able to help. We changed her diet, as someone had told us that corn syrup increased brain activity. I was diligently keeping track of each and every seizure with all of these changes we were trying. I was grateful to the Lord, who was giving me the ability to trust in Him for His perfect healing and time.

Basketball season transitioned to baseball and then to softball season. Since it was just me at home with Rich in New Mexico, all the kids came to all of the games, even Grace. We were at the ballfield many evenings and weekends for practices, games, and tournaments. The fields were several miles from where we lived. Grace enjoyed getting out of the house. She had a three-year-old friend from church whose big sister played on Megan's softball team. She enjoyed the interaction with her as well as many other children.

One of the many late nights at the beginning of April, I was driving the kids home after the game when Grace started seizing in the van. I could tell quickly that it was not one of her small seizures. I pulled the van over to the side of the country highway, jumped out quickly and got Grace out of her car seat and into my arms. I was hoping that the fresh night air would be enough to bring the seizure to a stop, but it was not. Eric, Ethan, and Megan sat in the van with the door open while I stood in the ditch rocking Grace from side to side. I started out singing and then went on to praying and pleading with God to help her seizure stop. The many cars that had left the same ballpark all zoomed by as if they did not even notice us. I turned my face away from the kids so they would not see my tears. The seizure seemed like it would never end. I knew some of the kids were starting to cry in the van. I'd tried to encourage them that it would be over soon, but they were afraid. We were all very afraid. Finally, after about ten minutes, the seizure stopped. It had not been our first ten-minute seizure, but it had been our first one in the ditch on the side of a highway with no one stopping to help us or even ask if we were okay. This was a situation that I did not want to be in again.

I called the neurologist the next day and we started making a plan to put Grace on yet another seizure medication. I hated to do it. These were such difficult decisions to make. She was already on three antiseizure medications. I knew increasing her meds or dosages would make her very tired, give her more secretions, and her smiling personality might possibly slip away from us. But I felt like it was our only choice. I just hoped that it would be a solution that we could stop eventually. It's not that I couldn't handle the seizures anymore, but what if the next time she didn't come out of it? What if we had lost her that night in the ditch or what about the next time it happened? We had to get her seizures under control.

On April 10, soon after Grace's third birthday, we saw some positive changes in her seizure activity. God had directed us to a new medication as well as a magnetic mattress—a mattress pad with magnets in it that are supposed to aid in healing. It was difficult to know which one worked or if it was both, but God knew and He allowed us to be strong enough to keep trying, to persevere until we were able to find something that truly helped Grace.

So, as I think back to those questions at the beginning:

Was I strong enough on my own? No, definitely not.

Could I be strong enough on my own? No, definitely not.

Did I want to be strong enough? Yes, I definitely did.

I came to realize that the only way that I could be strong enough physically, emotionally, spiritually, and mentally was to be broken before my Lord and Savior, Jesus Christ. I could try to do things in my own power and strength, but I would fail. I would stumble and I would fall. I know that I was not anywhere near perfect in my walk with Christ, so how could I be strong enough? I should have prayed more, searched God's Word more, sought His healing for Grace so much more, and asked for wisdom so much more than I did. I did do these things often but I will always feel like I should have done more. In my frailty and my weakness, in my ever-so-tired physical body, in my limited and stretched-beyond-measure of free time, Christ still proved Himself all powerful, all knowing, and always present in our lives. Nothing escaped His eyes. He saw it all, the unending trips to the emergency room, doctor's visits, hospital stays, every seizure—especially the ones that I could not see—every dose of medication given through the feeding tube, every UTI and the onsets of pneumonia, RSV, and C-Diff. He knew when it was a stomach virus and when it was just gas or constipation. He knew the reason for every fever. He saw her joy, kicking and chatting away in the middle of the night. He knew how much she was loved and how much she loved us, even when we couldn't always tell. He knew the words she was never able to say but was thinking. He knew when she was fearful and the many times she was so brave. He knew when I was too tired to keep my eyes open and He gave me strength to be awake multiple times night after night after night. He saw it all and gave me strength through it all. He heard me cry out and spoke to my heart to reassure me of His presence over and over and over again. He gave me the strength physically to carry her and lift her kid-cart/wheelchair in and out of our minivan in spite of my back issues. He gave me the strength to be mentally sharp with the doctors and the nurses to make sure they knew all of Grace's history, to ask the questions that would get her the help she needed in different situations. He directed us to the right doctors and hospitals and staff each time so Grace would get the help she needed to bring healing and keep her alive. He made her and knew every little part in her body that was not made normal according to the doctors, but God made her strong enough to live in spite of the abnormalities. Was I strong enough on my own? No, but I could definitely be strong enough if I clung on to Jesus.

2 Corinthians 12:9–10, "But he said to me, "My grace is sufficient for you, for my power is made perfect in weakness. Therefore I will boast all the more gladly about my weaknesses, so that Christ's power may rest on me. That is why, for Christ's sake, I delight in weakness, in insults, in hardship, in persecutions, in difficulties. For when I am weak, then I am strong."

I simply needed to acknowledge my weakness and ask Him for strength, and He would give it in abundance. There is so much power in the precious name of Jesus, all we have to do is say His name. It gives peace and strength. Yes, I was as strong as I needed to be, because of my relationship with Christ. I didn't need to worry about the future or what was to come. He would give strength for each day as it came. That was all I needed!

Grandma Lundt

Grandma Widman

Grandpa Lundt

Grandpa Widman at the park with us

Miss Bonnie - Texas Grandma

6

Beauty from the Ashes

John 10:10, "The thief comes only to steal and kill and destroy; I have come that they may have life, and have it to the full."

Have you ever gone through a learning and growing experience, perhaps even a painful one, thinking that it was to prepare you for something? That it could be something brought on by yourself, another person, or even the Lord? Only to find out that what you thought the preparation was for, was actually for something entirely different?

Ever since Grace's prenatal diagnosis, I had thought that I was struggling through the grieving process over and over in anticipation of her imminent death. I knew that God was constantly reminding me that she was not my own, that she was His. Grace was not even partially mine; she was created by Him and for Him; 100 percent His and His alone. All the time, effort, energy, love, and compassion that I had put into her since the day I found out I was pregnant did not make her mine to claim.

Each hospitalization was teaching me to give Grace over to God. Each day was teaching me to trust God's ways, His timing, and His plans instead of my own. I had to! I had grown to see how, as much as we women want to control everything around us—our husbands, our children, what our life looks like on the outside as well as on the inside—we truly don't have that control. Oh, it may look like it for a while, especially when our children are young. We can tell them what clothes to wear, cut or fix their hair as we desire, even get them to obey and behave the way we desire. But that does not last. They eventually grow into strong children or teenagers who desire to make their own decisions. They may not want to look the way we want them to, much less act, speak, or behave as we desire. With our husbands, we try to influence the way they dress by buying them clothes, or perhaps we make sure our house looks just so, or that we go to the right church. Whether or not they go along with it, these things may make us feel like we are in control of our world.

But with Grace there was no control from day one. What the doctors had prepared me for on the day of her birth, did not happen. I was incredibly grateful that God had complete control on that day and on all the days that followed after we brought her home. After that, as you have realized by reading this, even though I may have made plans for most days, many of those days my plans were changed. No one plans to bring a baby home on hospice. No one plans for their baby to be on a feeding tube. No one plans for aspiration pneumonia. No one plans for seizures to start, even when you know they are likely to come. God was continuing to show me that nothing truly was in my control, but that it was in His. I could trust Him. He would walk with me through whatever came my way, no matter how painful it was.

In Grace's first year of life, Steven Curtis Chapman's adopted daughter, Maria, suffered a tragic death. As I later read his wife MaryBeth's book, *Choosing to See,* and listened to Steven's DVD, *Beauty will Rise,* over and over, I cried for their loss but I also grew through the grieving process as I grieved with them for their sweet Maria, as well as for the loss that I would one day face of my Grace. The rawness of the Chapmans' feelings and the honesty that they shared moved me and challenged me to see my future differently from what I thought it was to be. I would need to choose to see, just as they had, that God is faithful. Steven's song talks of being broken, bleeding, scared, and confused. It speaks of when God gives and when He takes away. I was choosing to believe that God was faithful. How amazing! What a proclamation to make out of your pain. A favorite song on his CD was "Beauty Will Rise." The chorus talks about beauty rising out of the ashes and dancing among the ruins because we know that joy is coming in the morning, just as it tells us in Psalm 30:5.

I knew that God would be all I would need when that most difficult day came. I knew that when I was unable to cope or go on, Christ would carry me through it. I was very certain that there would indeed be eternal life for Grace after her physical death, but I was not so certain about the physical life here on earth for me after Grace's death. I was very unsure of moving on through life without her, but I knew that I would be able to with God's help. I knew that there would be beauty after death. I had indeed learned a lot. I had grown a lot.

I did not expect, though, that what God was preparing me for through this painful experience was not Grace's death. It wasn't anyone's death, at least not yet. From out of nowhere in 2010 came a death, a very tragic death, a kind of death that I didn't see coming because I was not looking for it. My focus was not on it, as it should have been. The death that I am referring to was the death of our marriage.

I am sure there were many signs I might have seen if I'd been alert to them, but I was distracted, very distracted. Even as I was busy watching Grace so diligently to prevent her death, my marriage was dying right in front of me, and I didn't see it happening. I knew, especially since the diagnosis during our pregnancy with Grace, that Rich and I had started to drift apart and had been seeking support from other people. We never really fought. There were no major disagreements or arguing—maybe those would have shown me some red flags to watch out for—but there was tension present at times. I felt pressure to be more than I was or more than I felt that I could be, the need to be perfect, and I knew I was not. With that pressure, I struggled with fear,

fear of my own husband, who had never done anything to warrant it. He was not aggressive in any way and had never yelled at me! I think my fear was of him being unhappy with me, angry with me, disappointed in me. I was a peacemaker, a conflict avoider. I would do or agree to almost anything to avoid an argument. I knew for years that Rich had always wanted our relationship to be more than just about the kids. He wanted "us" to have something worth looking forward to when the kids were no longer at home. I tried to make time for us and develop us, but when kids came along and especially when Grace came along, the "us" got left behind many times.

I remember one conversation that will forever be etched in my brain. Rich was sitting on the loveseat and I was sitting on the couch next to it holding Grace. It seemed like our normal night. The other kids were all in bed and we were just watching TV and having a little conversation, something that had become rare. His hours for work were very long and the brief time he was home I was usually taking care of the kids or doing Grace's medicine or other needs. On this particular night, Rich looked at me and said, "She's your number 1, isn't she?" I was a bit taken aback. We hadn't had a deep conversation in a long time, and now this question? It had been a tough couple of years. I looked at him with tears in my eyes and replied, "I know she is, but I don't know how to change it."

It was obvious to me at that time that Rich was unhappy, but I honestly didn't know what to do to change how I felt. I didn't know what to say to explain it or make him feel better. Our conversation ended, when truly that should have been the beginning of our talking and working together to understand each other and how to make our marriage better. Instead, I kept my feelings and thoughts to myself, just as I did after Grace's diagnosis, fearful that Rich wouldn't understand or that our thoughts would be too far apart from each other's to make anything work. I didn't explain to him that I felt like Grace's length of life depended on me, that I needed to give 150 percent energy, focus, and attention to her or we would lose her sooner somehow. She would die! He wasn't watching Grace every day; he was barely there. The rotating team of nurses was not there continually either, and no one knew Grace like I did. Grace was mostly unable to communicate. What she did communicate were very quiet moans or talking sounds and facial expressions if her medications were not making her too sleepy. I could read her every move, sound, and breath, and even then, I still missed things! Unlike in Omaha, where I had multiple friends and family who were at our house often, people I could talk to, share my concerns with, and pray with, in San Antonio I was very much alone most of the time. I don't mean to say that I did not have support. I did—wonderful people from church and school—but those close relationships take time to grow roots that are deep. We had only been in San Antonio for two years and now we were moving. I don't think Rich knew the intensity of the pressure I put on myself. How could he when I didn't share it with him?

In February of 2010, David Crowder came to town for a concert. I didn't know if I should spend the money on it since I knew Rich would not be able to be in town to go with me, but the kids all wanted to go and Rich said that we should. Of course, halfway through the concert, the kids were tired and ready to leave, but I held them off for just a couple more songs. The band finally played "How He Loves." What an awesome worship experience to have the whole audience singing along with him, "O, how He loves us." Then he had us personalize it and sing "O, how He loves me." I had no idea how singing that truth over and over again that night would truly impact me. When you know that you are loved by the Creator of the whole universe, by Almighty God, you are much more likely to trust Him when you are not sure you can trust anyone else. This is one of the truths that I would need to cling to in the days and months to come.

Rich had already left for his job in Albuquerque, and once again I found myself with four children, one who was medically fragile with frequent hospital stays, while I was also trying to sell a house. I was so busy trying to keep up with all the kids' activities, doctors' appointments, and unexpected hospital stays and illnesses, that Rich and I rarely talked each day. He hadn't felt that he was the priority before and it just grew worse.

After about five months of Rich being in Albuquerque and barely making it home for any visits, our marriage crashed. We both finally realized that we were a mess, bigger than I ever imagined we could be. This had not just happened overnight. It did not just come from one bad disagreement. It hadn't just happened because we now had a medically fragile child in the mix. It had been a slow fade into making choices that led us our separate ways. Satan had been planting thoughts in our minds that appeared to be truth but indeed were not. Looking back, I do believe it was inevitable, and the pressures of the circumstances of our lives sped up the process. Our counselor had shared the statistic with us that couples with a special needs child have a divorce rate of 75 percent. The death that God had been truly preparing me for was the death of our marriage.

***

We were just a few months short of celebrating our twentieth anniversary. How could it have gotten so bad? Rich was to the point where he truly thought we would both be happier if we just weren't together. He was tired of being so far down the list of my priorities. He felt we had no connection anymore and that he had just become a paycheck to me. He thought that the only reason I wanted us together was to make the family picture complete. It broke my heart to realize that Rich felt that way, but I knew that I no longer felt the deep, passionate love for him that I had years ago. I didn't even feel friendship at this point. Where had it gone? When did I lose it? I knew that when we had said our vows I had meant them to last forever, even if the fire wasn't burning very hot or bright anymore.

As evening came on that horrible day, words were becoming less. We searched for some middle ground where we could be together and we decided to watch the movie *Fireproof*. We had received the DVD a year or two before as a gift and had never watched it. The movie was about a marriage headed for divorce when a forty-day experiment called "The Love Dare" challenged the husband in the movie to make the effort to love again. It was a very good movie, and particularly eye opening for us in that moment of our life. We realized we had stopped pursuing each other long before. This was another "God moment" to me. I don't believe it was an accident that we had not watched that movie until that night. God knew when we would be most receptive to it. He knew some of the songs in that movie would speak volumes to both Rich and to me. God knows our needs before they even exist and He meets them in His perfect timing.

We were at a crossroads; decisions had to be made and changes had to happen. We could not just continue on the way we had been living. Would we continue with the plan, sell the house, and move to Albuquerque; or would we call it quits like so many others, with Rich moving on to Albuquerque and the kids and I either staying put or move back to the Midwest. Somewhere along my path, the words "obedience brings blessing" had been ingrained in my brain. I just knew that, biblically, they would hold true. As I prayed and cried out to the Lord at this time, "obedience brings blessing" just kept ringing through my head. I absolutely knew that God did not want us to become another statistic in the rising divorce rate in the society that we lived in. That was not God's best for anyone, no matter what Satan was trying to tell us.

Rich and I both had a lot of hurts and problems that we had been sweeping under the carpet. They could not stay there any longer. They had to be dealt with. So, as we talked that day, Rich asked me if I thought we could make it work. I honestly did not have much love in my heart, but I told him that the one thing I had truly come to believe was that God could do the impossible. I had definitely seen that during my pregnancy with Grace and in her life. If I truly believed that, then I truly had to believe that He could help us to love each other again. He could bind up the brokenhearted. He could heal our wounds.

Rich and I were both very broken. Our marriage was dead. There was anger, bitterness, unforgiveness, resentment, selfishness, and pride in both of us. Those feelings had built up a very large wall between us that would need to be taken down if our marriage was to survive. Many of the memories and the thoughts of what had been good in our marriage were now tainted with this darkness that had been cast on it. All that I thought was good seemed lost. I told Rich that if we were going to try to save our marriage, we had to do it God's way. I was scared to death that he would just say no, that it wasn't worth the work, but he agreed.

At that point we started on the long journey. Not a journey to what we once had and then lost— that was not going to be good enough. That would not hold in the storms. It had to be better and stronger than before. It had to be built on the foundation of Christ first for both of us, then each other, then our children. Once again, God gave me songs that spoke truth into my heart. I truly don't understand how God miraculously made these songs popular on my Christian radio stations at the right time every time. My only explanation is just that is what God does . . . because He can!

The song "No Matter What" by Kerrie Roberts was painfully true. I did not understand why God was allowing this to happen to our marriage. I had grown up in a home where, honestly, I never saw my parents argue or fight, and they were fine. Rich and I were not arguing and fighting, and yet things were anything but fine. I did know as this song said, that no matter what happened or didn't happen in our marriage from that day forward, I would still need and love my God.

"Before the Morning" by Josh Wilson was another very encouraging song that gave me hope. It reminded me that I cannot see everything. I cannot see the end from the beginning like God can. It was hard to imagine that there would be joy at the end of all this pain. Where was God and why had He allowed this? As I kept singing this truth and reminding myself of the truth of God's Word, I knew there was a bigger picture that we cannot see and God could bring a better ending. It was unfathomable how God could fade this pain into memory just by seeing His glory, but I knew all things were possible with God. I just needed to press on and keep fighting the good fight.

Honestly, the death of our marriage really shook me. There were days and moments when I just had to tell myself to breathe, when all I could say in my prayers was the precious name of Jesus. There were days when the nurse would come in the morning and I would go back up to my bedroom, curl up in my bed, and cry or sleep because I couldn't do anything else. I remember one day I was at a stoplight waiting to cross the very busy Highway 281. For a split second, as I watched the big semi-trucks passing quickly in front of me, I thought it would be better to just pull out in front of one, then my kids came to my mind. As crushed as my spirit truly was, I could not hurt them that way. It was a comfort for me to know that in my weak state, the Holy Spirit was interceding for me, for us.

Romans 8:26, "In the same way, the Spirit helps us in our weakness. We do not know what we ought to pray for, but the Spirit himself intercedes for us with groans that words cannot express."

Even though it appeared like Rich and I were going to give it an honest effort, there was a lot of pain and fear in it all. This really knocked us both down to the ground. There were many tears shed. I tried to hold it together when I was in front of the kids. We really tried to protect them from all of it, but I know that my heart was an emotional mess. To be honest, I was told by someone that I had confided in that this was just too much for me to bear. She meant that, with all that I had gone through and was still continuing to go through with Grace, adding my marriage problems on top of that was more than I should have to bear. There were many days when I could have easily taken up that cross. It did seem like too much. I had done some scripture memory long ago in Omaha with Cheryl. Somewhere in our last move my 3 x 5 cards of verses had been lost, but the Lord was good to bring them back to my sight during this time, reminding me of the promises I had learned long ago.

1 Peter 5:10, "And the God of all grace, who called you to his eternal glory in Christ, after you have suffered a little while, will himself restore you and make you strong, firm and steadfast."

Psalm 138:7–8, "Though I walk in the midst of trouble, you preserve my life; you stretch out your hand against the anger of my foes, with your right hand you save me. The Lord will fulfill his purpose for me; your love, O Lord, endures forever—do not abandon the works of your hands."

One day when I was driving in my van with Grace on the way home from a doctor's appointment, the precious song "I Lift My Hands" by Chris Tomlin came on the radio and, with tears rolling down my cheeks, I realized that I needed to lift my hands. Even though my spirit was crushed, I needed to restate out loud to Christ and to myself that "I Did Believe Again . . . I Still Believed."

I do believe that one thing that helped restore our marriage was that we both took our share of responsibility for the broken state of our marriage. We had both made mistakes. We had both hurt each other in very different ways, but we accepted our roles in it, asked for forgiveness, gave forgiveness. Did you know that sometimes we need to give forgiveness over and over and over? As much as we may desire for it to be said and done once, our sin nature does not always allow it to work that way. It is too easy to hang on to the hurt and pain that causes bitterness and anger. I am so thankful that my God is not like me.

Colossians 2:13, "When you were dead in your sins and in the uncircumcision of your sinful nature, God made you alive with Christ." He forgave us all our sins, having canceled the charge of our legal indebtedness, which stood against us and condemned us; he has taken it away, nailing it to the cross.

We sought godly counseling separately and then together. This was vital to working through many of our issues. One thing Rich was told was to "lean in." He shared this with me and it became so helpful. We had been so hurt by each other that holding hands or even sitting next to each other was something that had to be intentional. It was not our desire to be close and lean in, but we kept doing it anyway. We were amazed that as our counseling progressed, the counselor pointed out the difference in our proximity to each other on the counseling couch. We had started at opposite ends of the couch. Each week as we were working toward the same goal together, the gap on the couch between us continued getting smaller. After only a few months of counseling, we were sitting next to each other on the couch holding hands.

***

There was one thing that I did right away and I am not sure if it was consciously or subconsciously, but I made an emotional break from Grace. I can't say that I intentionally set out to do it. I think God just did it for me. I could feel it happening over about a two-week period. Don't get me wrong. I still loved Grace, I took care of her, held her, and spent time with her, but I could definitely feel a shift in my priorities, loyalties, and first love. It is a very difficult thing to explain, but I could definitely feel it happening. During that time, I knew it was a necessity in restoring our marriage, but there was also part of me that was just brokenhearted. It was difficult. I had known for years that my priorities were to be God first, Richard second, and then my kids. Somewhere in the last few years, mine had become all jumbled together. My top priority varied according to the need at the time, and most of the time the need was Grace. I really have come to believe that God was working in my heart during this two-week time frame to "reset" me. It was not something that I set out to do, it just started happening. I knew our marriage was in such a critical state that drastic measures needed to be taken.

One thing Rich started doing fairly quickly after we all got to New Mexico was telling me how beautiful I was. I don't think this was counsel directed. He just started doing it, a lot. Honestly, I did not know how to receive it. He had never called me that before, and I am not sure anyone had. I had never realized the power of a single word like that before. Being beautiful was never at the top of my list of important things to achieve. I always tried to look nice but did not consider myself a beautiful person. I was trying desperately to come out of a season of feeling unloved and rejected, but I could hardly believe that he meant it or that it was even true. Nevertheless, his persistence in telling me did start to build me up again. Eventually, I was able to start receiving his compliments as truth. This next song came out in September of 2010. A coincidence? I don't think so. I believe that God has everything planned clear down to the music on your radio if you are walking with Him. The song "Beautiful" by MercyMe gave me new insight into who I truly was in Christ. I felt anything but beautiful. Yet this song told me I was treasured, sacred, His, beautiful. Singing this song out loud gave me strength deep in my soul to keep fighting, to keep working. God's beautiful would shine through.

I don't mean to sound like I did everything right, or even that what Rich and I did was the key to making a marriage survive. I definitely did and said many things that added to the difficulty of what had to be worked through. We were not even close to perfect in how we handled it all. I am simply trying to share some of the positive steps that I think helped pave the road for us to get back to each other, back to us.

Another thing that we were not perfect on, but tried to be wise about after getting counsel, was that we tried to keep our marriage struggles fairly private. There were just a faithful few we shared any of this with. A faithful friend told me, the more people you tell, the more people will have to work through it with you. It was hard enough working through our stuff with just the two of us. I cannot imagine if everyone else knew and had to work through hard feelings and forgiveness too! We had our few for support, literally a couple for me and a couple for Rich. We needed that support as well as the brutal honesty they gave us. My support did not always give me the exact words I wanted to hear, but she was honest. She also gave me Scripture and the encouragement to persevere. I knew that they were supporting me in prayer daily, not just once a day, but many moments of each day. I know those prayers were holding me up.

Both Rich and I realized that the time apart on our moves had definitely taken a toll. I had always wanted to be the supportive wife in his career, so I tried not to complain about the way we did our moves. He was doing his best to provide for our family, and doing an awesome job, but it also had great pressure. He usually would have to report for any new job within two weeks, and I would stay back with the kids until the house was sold. He would fly back for an occasional weekend, and I would do my best to keep everything afloat: getting kids to their activities, school, doctor's appointments, church, as well as keeping the house clean and ready for a showing at the last possible second. I had it down to a science. The kids all knew their roles when I received a call that the house was to show. They would clean up their things and help with whatever else needed to be done. We would load Grace and all her supplies in the van with at least one sibling in there also to help watch her. Sometimes, depending on how frantic I was feeling at the time, I would just send all four of them straight to the van. I would do my last once over, making sure every toilet was flushed, all the toys were picked up, the dishes were done, counters wiped off, the dirty laundry basket usually just went out to the van, and then I would systematically vacuum every room in the house as I carefully backed out of each room leaving no footprints in the house. I then turned on every light in the house. This may seem extreme, but that way, when I came back after the showing, I had immediate feedback that someone had looked at the house by the footprints that were now in the rooms as well as the lights that usually were shut off out of habit in some rooms as they exited.

For some moves, this job seemed endless, and leaving San Antonio was one of them. We would carefully pay attention to any comments people left, but unfortunately with our San Antonio home, most of the comments were about things that were out of our control. There was a water tower behind our neighbor's backyard. We liked it there because it meant we had no backyard neighbors and that meant privacy. Unfortunately, others did not see it like we did. While I did that on my end, Rich worked hard at his new location getting to know his new staff and hotel, often working long hours. He would often live at the hotel, which seemed nice in my imagination. But for him, working and living at the same place made for many long days, weeks, and months. It was lonely for him being apart from his family for so long. While our roles were very different and seemed very necessary, I don't think either one of us could truly put ourselves in the other's shoes. God's Word is clear in Genesis 2:24, Mark 10:8, and Ephesians 5:31 that the two will become one and the husband will hold fast to his wife. We had been making choices that were preventing that.

We realized quite quickly that if we were going to get on the right path, we had to be very deliberate in pursuing each other, which meant we had to make the necessary effort to be together. You can only do so much toward repairing a broken marriage over the phone. We did indeed start burning up the phone lines, but we also became intentional in seeing each other. Two weeks after our marriage crashed, I flew out to Albuquerque. This was something that had seemed impossible before. It was costly and there was no possible way to leave four kids behind, especially Grace! But I knew I needed to show Rich that he was that important to me and I needed to make it happen, so Eric, Ethan, and Megan all went to their best friends' homes. As for Grace, she was a little more complex. I had two wonderful ladies from the church come to stay at the house with her for the weekend. They were there to love on her and be her guardians in case of an emergency. Then I also had my wonderful day nurse and night nurse rearrange their schedules so one of them was there around the clock the whole time. Gracie was totally covered, and I got on a plane.

Getting off that plane in Albuquerque was a bit scary. We were only two weeks out from our crash, the wounds were not scarred over yet, not even close; it felt like they were open and still gushing with blood. We both still had a lot of hurt, anger, resentment, and much more. The pain from almost losing our marriage had literally made me sick for the last couple of weeks, and I had lost some weight. It didn't seem to matter if I ate or not, the pounds just kept coming off. I don't think either of us were sure that it would really work. But it was Albuquerque, New Mexico. I had always felt like Albuquerque was our Promised Land! It had been sweet the first time we lived there ten years ago, and I truly believed that God hand-picked that city for us to rebuild our marriage. He would make all things new! After all, that is what God does. It's His specialty.

Revelation 21:5, "I am making everything new!"

2 Corinthians 5:17, "Therefore, if anyone is in Christ, he is a new creation; the old has gone, the new has come!"

That weekend together was the next step in the right direction. Yes, it was hard. Some very tough conversations were had, but at least they were starting to be had. We drove around Albuquerque looking at possible neighborhoods to live in. We road-tripped up to Santa Fe for a night away, and we went to the church in Albuquerque that Rich had already fallen in love with. The worship and pastor were both amazing! The size made me nervous. We hadn't been in a megachurch before, but I knew that I needed to let Rich lead in finding our church this time. He had already found one where he connected with the pastor; that was a huge blessing right there. I could see that God was working in Rich's life. There were songs that Rich would play for me that were speaking to him in amazing ways. I had always prayed that Rich would be the spiritual leader of our family, and now I was beginning to see that emerge in him. Would I be strong enough to fight through those rough waters with him to get there? It would never have been the way that I would have chosen for it to happen, but only God knew him well enough to plan the right way to bring it to pass. I flew home with a bit of renewed hope, hope that God could do the impossible! He could save our marriage, but would it truly be good?

***

We decided that weekend that we were done being apart. The kids had done well that weekend. Miraculously, about the same time our marriage started heading in the right direction of healing, so did Grace's seizures. We had been given a magnet mattress and a magnet necklace that we started using. Her seizures quickly went from fifty a day to twenty a day. I arrived home from that weekend and immediately planned to leave the next Thursday for New Mexico for a long weekend, this time driving with all four kids. It was the beginning of May. Soon the kids would be out of school and we could be in New Mexico a lot more. We kept praying for our home to sell and trusted that God had our future in His hands.

Jeremiah 29:11, "'For I know the plans I have for you,' declares the Lord, 'plans to prosper you and not to harm you, plans to give you hope and a future.'"

I drove that road from San Antonio, Texas, to Albuquerque, New Mexico, several times that summer. It was 11 ½ hours! We would go on a weekend and stay for a week through the next weekend. Then we would come back home to check on the house, do doctors' appointments, and start getting the house ready for the move. The couple times that we were at home in San Antonio, Grace did end up in the hospital, but thankfully with nothing too major—a UTI and a sinus infection. For most people those are not big illnesses, but for Grace it was different. This time they could only be treated with IV antibiotics, so into the hospital she went. Eventually, they were able to put a PICC line in Grace's upper arm, and they trained me how to do IV antibiotics so we could take her home.

Most trips went really well. Our children were becoming professionals at road-tripping! They each had their fun bag packed to keep them busy in the van. Megan always liked to play with Grace, and Grace was an excellent little traveler as well. We had to do our normal pit stops for restroom breaks and gas, and of course we also had to add in stops for diaper changes and meds and feedings. The kids and I were all feeling like our hearts were already in New Mexico. We couldn't wait to get there to be with Richard in person.

Of course, the kids loved the stays in the hotel. They loved the food, the pool, and living the vacation life! Even though the kids were there, Rich and I were managing to get to our counseling and work on our marriage. We were learning how to communicate again. On one of our visits, I was able to go on an early morning hike up into the Sandia Mountains with some people Rich knew. It was a beautiful morning and quite a challenge since I had never been much of a hiker. As we were hiking, I was getting to know the people I was hiking with. When I told them about our medically fragile child who'd had lots of hospital stays and needed lots of doctors, they commented that they didn't think that Albuquerque was a very good place to move to. They wondered why we would leave all the good doctors in San Antonio to come to Albuquerque. According to them, the only good doctor in Albuquerque was a urologist. I just had to smile and laugh to myself as I told them that the only real specialist Grace still needed was a urologist for her surgery! Once again, God was showing me that He and only He had everything in control. He knew our need and met it! How amazing was He?

Rich and I had decided that doing life apart was not the right choice anymore, even if financially it did not seem possible. We decided that we would start renting a house in New Mexico on August 1, even if our house in San Antonio was not sold. We knew it was God's best plan for us as a married couple to be together, and that He would provide the way. So we found the house to rent, started looking into schools, started looking for doctors, and applying for Medicaid. Did I know with absolute certainty that our marriage was going to survive by the time the kids and I moved to Albuquerque on August 1? Absolutely not. I don't think Rich was totally convinced that it was going to survive either. We just had to trust that if we kept taking steps of obedience, God would honor that and provide the strength and the support we needed to sustain our marriage. We knew He could. His Word is full of verses in which He not only heals but restores and redeems.

Isaiah 61:1–4,

> The Spirit of the sovereign LORD is on me, because the Lord has anointed me to preach good news to the poor. He has sent me to bind up the brokenhearted, to proclaim freedom for the captives, and release from darkness for the prisoners, to proclaim the year of the Lord's favor and the day of vengeance of our God, to comfort all who mourn, and provide for those who grieve in Zion—to bestow on them a crown of beauty instead of ashes, the oil of gladness instead of mourning, and a garment of praise instead of a spirit of despair. They will be called oaks of righteousness, a planting of the Lord for the display of his splendor. They will rebuild the ancient ruins and restore the places long devastated for generations.

Psalm 72:14, "He will rescue them from oppression and violence, for precious is their blood in his sight."

Galatians 4:4–5, "But when the time had fully come, God sent his Son, born of a woman, born under law, to redeem those under law, that we might receive the full rights of sons."

I had always heard the line that "God loves us too much to leave us the way we are." I am not sure I had ever experienced it, though, in such a big way, but that is what God was doing. He saw a marriage of two people, two people He loved very much, two people He had ordained to be together, and He saw that their marriage wasn't good enough. It was pretty good for years, only okay for the last couple, but did God really want us to settle for pretty good or okay? Did He really want infection boiling under the surface until it became a deadly infection? Only God knew that right remedy to bring true healing to our marriage, to us. If God's plan for our lives was for our good and to bring glory to Himself, how was that going to happen if we were settling for just okay? Or perhaps barely surviving? I kept thinking back to the day when Rich and I got married. God knew that we needed each other to be complete in Him. He designed and strengthened us both for the many different circumstances and difficulties that would come our way, and that definitely included our marriage crashing. He put us together with the knowledge that we would not throw in the towel and quit no matter how painful and difficult it became. He knew we would look to Him as we fought for our marriage.

Something that kept running through my head was the phrase, *God is worthy*. The more it ran through my brain, the more it came to life in my head and heart. It started coming out as *"God is worth it."* If my goal was to glorify God in my life, to bring Him praise, if He truly was my King of Kings and Lord of Lords and I was living for Him, then this pain that He allowed was worth it. As I turned those words over and over in my mind, I realized that Rich was worth it also. Our marriage was worth it. Before God, I had pledged my love to Rich in marriage almost twenty years before. I had chosen to love him on days he was not very loveable, just as he had done for me. In that many years of marriage, there are going to be days when you have to choose to love your spouse even though you do not always feel it. I had prayed for Rich to be my spiritual leader as well as the spiritual leader of our family. Wouldn't it be worth it if God chose to do that at this time in our life? The growth that I needed to go through to have a healthy marriage was also worth it! If something is worth it, then it is also worth fighting for. Warren Barfield's song, "Love Is Not a Fight," from the movie *Fireproof*, said it so beautifully. Love is not a fight, but it's something worth fighting for. Every drive to Albuquerque, every phone call, every counseling session, every bit of forgiveness and compassion, was all fighting for our marriage, and our marriage was worth every bit of it.

Somehow very early on in our marriage crashing, the song "Beautiful, Beautiful" by Francesca Battistelli reached my soul and spirit. I could be sobbing through the brokenness and still be singing this song in my kitchen at the top of my lungs with some joy inside that I couldn't understand or explain. I truly believe that the only reason I could see a glimpse of that joy was because I knew that God was working. He would change us. He would indeed make Rich, myself, and our marriage all beautiful. The ugliness of where we were at that moment would dissipate. I didn't know how long it would take, but I knew that beautiful would be on the other end, and beauty would rise from the ashes of this broken marriage.

7

Build Us Back

After our many trips back and forth between San Antonio, Texas, and Albuquerque, New Mexico, that summer of 2010, we were definitely ready to move to Albuquerque. Rich and I were continuing to see the counselor each time we were there. He was helping us to communicate much better. We had a lot to work through. He had started by giving us simple tips such as to lean in, which simply meant to move in physically closer—even when we did not especially feel it—sit closer, reach for that hand to hold, don't be afraid of the closeness. We definitely would not always feel like it. Much of our love for each other had been tainted, seemingly destroyed and crushed. As we learned to communicate again and how to meet each other's needs, leaning in would begin to feel more natural once again.

When we began our summer visits, I think we were both skeptical as to whether the counseling and effort we were putting in would actually work, if we truly had what it took to put our marriage back together. We knew it needed to be different. We both had changes that we needed to make. With each step, we were not just moving closer to living in Albuquerque, but we were moving closer to each other. Excitement as well as anxiety was growing. Could we really do this? Once again, fear crept into my spirit and I had to trust that if we were obedient to God in our efforts for our marriage, He would come through and bless it.

Our home in San Antonio had still not sold; not only were we taking a huge leap of faith where our marriage was concerned, but we'd stretched ourselves very thin where our finances were concerned. We would be taking on two house payments, which meant that we were not able to put all of our children in a Christian school right away. This would be a sacrifice the whole family would be participating in. We had not heard good things about the Albuquerque public school system but did not see any other way. We could afford for only one child to go to Christian school so we chose Eric. He was the oldest and we thought he would be in the most difficult position in the public school as a new student. Ethan and Megan would have to start in the public school. Megan was only in third grade so she did pretty well but she struggled with the teacher using God's name in vain and asked us when she could go to the Christian school. Ethan seemed to have a more difficult time in the sixth grade, the first year of middle school. About a week into the school year, Rich was speaking with his dad who offered to loan us the money for Ethan's first semester at Hope Christian School. We accepted his gracious offer and the transition was quickly made. This made a huge difference for Ethan. What a blessing that was for our family.

We moved into our new rented home on August 1, 2010. The kids loved the adventure of exploring our new home and surroundings. We were back in the land of the brown—brown sand, brown rocks, and every shade of brown homes everywhere you looked. I realize it doesn't sound appealing, but we loved the different landscapes, plants, and even the many lizards. We especially loved the mountains and they became an instant and constant reminder to me of where my help was. A verse I had learned long before came to my mind every time I went on a run and had them in my sights. I did not have friends in Albuquerque—that would take time. I had my family, which was still a bit shaky. This verse reminded me constantly that I had my God. He had been my friend for years. He had been my help in every other city we had lived in through every season of life and He would be my constant help here in Albuquerque as well. Albuquerque was full of hills, but you could always see the mountains. What a reminder.

Psalm 121:1–2, "I lift my eyes to the hills—where does my help come from? My help comes from the Lord, the Maker of heaven and earth."

The boys got right into football. It seemed like wherever we practiced we had the beautiful mountains in the background. We loved seeing the hot air balloons each morning. Many landed quite close behind our house. We jumped right into the new church that Rich had found. Rich had told me over and over again how much he loved going there. Now I was able to see and experience it week after week with him. Our worship time became a time when Rich and I felt very close to each other and to our Savior. We were being challenged in ways we had not been for quite some time. We loved the worship music and were constantly downloading the new music we experienced at the church. Holding Rich's hand as we worshiped was a new experience of oneness that I don't believe we had ever experienced together. Sure, we had held hands before in a church service, but this time it was different. For the first time in a very long time, we were both aiming for the same goals. We jumped into a life group at Rich's direction. In the past I had been the one who pushed for it, but this time it was him. He knew we had a need for Christian fellowship and discipleship.

I was also blessed to find a wonderful ladies Bible study right away. I was still a bit of an emotional mess when I started going, but I knew I desperately needed the study and the fellowship of godly women. The study was in a home and I remember walking up to the front door thinking, *They have no idea what kind of a mess I am.* I was not only dealing with the pressures of four children—one of them a medically fragile toddler—and getting settled in a new town, but I was also recovering from the massive amount of emotional injury our marriage had left me in. I was healing day by day, but I had a long way to go. The Bible study I did with those ladies as well as the sharing and encouraging we did was making me stronger, helping me to focus on God's truth of what He was doing in our marriage instead of listening to Satan's lies. He had deceived us both for far too long. It was time to stop listening to him and focus on what God was doing. He was making all things new!

Isaiah 43:18–19, "Forget the former things; do not dwell on the past. See, I am doing a new thing! Now it springs up; do you not perceive it? I am making a way in the desert and streams in the wasteland."

He would rebuild the ruins.

All of those things were building us back. I remember the day we went to counseling and the counselor pointed out how, when we first started coming to him, we were sitting on opposite ends of the couch, arms crossed, very closed off. Then he pointed out how on that day we were sitting side by side—our legs were touching we were so close—and holding hands. And it wasn't because we were forcing ourselves to lean in any longer. We were definitely making progress. God was faithfully doing His thing, just as we had seen many times in the last two years. He was doing yet another miracle.

The counselor had told us that people who get divorced think they are taking the easy way out, but in fact, divorce was really just a quick fix to the immediate problems. It was not a long-term fix. The difficulties from a divorce last a very long time, perhaps a lifetime if there are children involved. While we were not getting the quick fix, God was definitely doing a miracle in helping us work through the process.

While all of this marriage rebuilding was going on, life just kept going! We were getting settled into our new home, the kids' new schools, and a new job for Rich. While many things were moving right along, we were still waiting: waiting for our home in San Antonio to sell and waiting for Grace to get on Medicaid. Yes, we still had insurance, but we knew that just one extended hospital stay would put us in great debt. We really didn't know how we were managing two house payments as well as one child in Christian school! God was providing. Our many faithful prayer warriors were all praying with us, not only for our home to sell and for Grace to be accepted on Medicaid, but also that she would not get sick and require a hospitalization and that our supply of medical necessities that we had brought from San Antonio would not run out. From all of our hospital stays in San Antonio, our supplies built up into extras. In Albuquerque we were living on our extras!

We did have an early trip to the ER and a hospital stay in September, but it was not Grace. It was Eric! He had been at football practice when he made a great tackle, but unfortunately another boy's hip had landed right on his arm, breaking both bones in his forearm. Thankfully surgery was not needed! I had learned some very helpful things from having Grace. Someone at practice had called 911 and they had Eric in an ambulance when Rich got to practice. When he called me to ask which hospital to go to, I quickly told him to get Eric out of the ambulance and I would come take him to the hospital. I knew that little ride would cost us at least a thousand dollars that we did not need to spend. I had seen enough medical bills to know that. I already knew the way to the children's hospital from an appointment with Grace's new pediatrician.

God was obviously taking care of our finances and choosing to bless us along the way. Grace had three UTI's from the beginning of August to the middle of October, but she did not need to be hospitalized for them.

We were blessed even before Grace got on Medicaid. A medical supply company that was eager to get in good standing with the hospital provided us with a pulse oximeter to keep at our home to monitor Grace's oxygen levels, oxygen to keep at home for emergency situations, and also a high frequency chest wall oscillation machine. We fondly called it the Shake 'n Bake machine. We would put this vest on Grace twice a day and it would gently shake her lung region to help prevent her lungs from getting pneumonia. The company did not charge us past what our insurance would pay and waited patiently for the Medicaid to kick in to pay off the rest of the account. What a huge blessing! By the end of November, Grace was officially accepted on New Mexico's Medicaid plan!

Our home sold in November that year, and though there were some complications on the buyer's end, it was in the process of being completely done and off our financial responsibility list. By second semester all the kids were able to be enrolled at Hope Christian School. As an added bonus, Hope Christian was close to where Rich worked and he enjoyed taking them all to school each day.

We definitely were seeing God's faithfulness and blessings on our family as we were working at building back our marriage and our family. We saw it in His provision in selling our home, Grace's Medicaid acceptance, and her good health until it came through, financial provision through two house payments, and our children doing well in the different schools they were now attending. We were able to enjoy family time at the many football games and practices, the hot air balloon festival, our times swimming or having breakfast at "Daddy's hotel" as the kids called it! The church and the Bible study groups we were attending also were definitely playing a big part in our healing and growth. God was taking two very broken people and rebuilding our relationship in the land that we had always loved. It was not yet all perfect; it would be a long process. But we could definitely see God's goodness oozing all over our lives together.

Psalm 27:13–14, "I am still confident of this: I will see the goodness of the LORD in the land of the living. Wait for the Lord; be strong and take heart and wait for the LORD."

This verse was so true for me. My belief in the Lord and His goodness and what I knew He could do drove me through the tougher days as we were still growing and healing. God's Word is just as true for us today as it was for those in the time of King David.

Exodus 33:19, "And the LORD said, 'I will cause all my goodness to pass in front of you, and I will proclaim my name, the Lord, in your presence. I will have mercy on whom I will have mercy, and I will have compassion on whom I will have compassion.'"

Grace

Grace, Cami, and Megan

Kids on couch

Cami and Grace at the pool

Balloon Festival

8

She's Yours, Lord

We were so grateful to have had a calm fall. God was so good to keep Grace healthy enough to stay out of the hospital and really keep our medical bills at a minimum until her Medicaid came through. We were truly blessed to be able to go back to the Midwest for Christmas. It had been a while since we had seen both of our families. We were not gone too long before we returned to Albuquerque. We had not been on Medicaid for very long so we had not received any nursing care yet for Grace. So I was mom/nurse non-stop 24/7, which I truly enjoyed, but it was also very exhausting at times. There were some mornings when I would get up to do her 6:00 a.m. medications and if she was still sleepy, I would go back to bed to try to catch a few more moments of sleep myself.

December 30, 2010, was one of those mornings when I did manage to go back to sleep. At one point I heard Megan get out of bed and go downstairs. Grace was quiet so I laid in bed a little longer relishing the quiet time. Megan was downstairs with her brothers watching television. I finally decided to roll out of bed and go check on my baby girl. I walked down the hall and into her room only to see her face down in her bed. This may not seem bad for a normal two-year-old, but Grace was not a normal two-year-old. She did not have the neck strength to pick up her head and turn it. Her head was not turned to the right or the left, but straight down into the comforter. I couldn't believe my eyes. Grace had not rolled over for months! We had her in her SleepSafe bed, but the magnet mattress was on top of the original mattress and did not line up with the width of the bed. It left a little less than a foot of space where there was a space a little lower with a comforter in that space. Every night we put Grace to bed on the opposite side of the bed to lay and she never moved from that space. Now here she was face down in a comforter in the lower section where she was not able to get out, lying seemingly lifeless before me. I rolled her over immediately and I honestly thought she was dead. Her color was not good. I thought I had lost her. In my shock I gave her two rescue breaths. I know I wasn't thinking clearly, because even with my many training classes of CPR, this time I did not even put my mouth over hers. Thankfully she took a big breath right after I did that. I yelled for Eric to bring me my phone so I could call 911. I was so scared and frantic. Then I put the Ambu Bag on her. This is a hand-held, self-inflating bag used to provide positive ventilation to patients who are not breathing or not breathing adequately. The firemen got there fairly quickly and I was still standing at Grace's bedside in my pajamas pumping air into Grace. The fireman took the Ambu Bag from me, telling me that I was not using it correctly and that it was not doing her any good. This was something given to me during one of our hospital stays, but no one had ever actually showed me how to use it. Later as I talked to the doctor, they said that it had done her some good because it was still pushing air into her lungs.

The paramedics quickly put Grace on oxygen. Her heart rate was at 200 when they arrived. I had called Rich to come home and be with the kids. I changed quickly after the paramedics arrived and went in the ambulance with Grace to the hospital. I was still very shaken and scared as we rode in the ambulance to the hospital. Grace was breathing but was still very out of it. As I was telling the story of what had happened, to the men in the ambulance, Grace's stats started looking better. I was still very fearful of any brain damage that might have occurred. If Grace had brain damage, we would most likely lose her entirely. With all of the seizure medications she was on, we were not able to see her full personality as it was. She was able to communicate with us and do certain things, and we were so thankful for every little aspect. Each little ability she had was HUGE to us! Thankfully a few hours after the incident as Grace was being monitored in the hospital, she started showing signs that she was still her sweet little self with no brain damage. We praised the Lord that she was still with us! I was so thankful that in my inadequacy in that fateful moment, God took over and let it be enough.

I would like to say that we all had a quick recovery from that fearful episode. Grace did! I, on the other hand, could not get that image out of my head—the image of my lifeless little girl with no breath in her. I would close my eyes at night and see her again and again. It did not escape my mind that if I'd stayed in bed just a little longer, she would not be with us anymore. My guilty thoughts of going back to bed that day, of not being more attentive, were beating me up. I knew and I am sure that God knew that I was not ready to lose Grace that day, not like that. I honestly don't know if I would have ever recovered from the guilt. I am so thankful that God knows me well enough not to have allowed that. I am not sure why that had to happen on that day. My only guess was that it was a big reminder of Grace's frailty and the fragility of her life. She was not strong bodied like my other children. Anything could take her life, even when we were not expecting it. We needed to treasure each day. We needed to enjoy each hug, each smile, each time we were able to hold her. Every moment with her was a gift.

We had a nice long run without a hospitalization, then on Monday, January 10, 2011, I took Grace in to be checked for a UTI. Sure enough, she had one and we had her on an antibiotic by that evening. Also on that Monday we were in for some routine tests for the kidney specialist that included an x-ray. That x-ray revealed that Grace had pneumatosis intestinalis, which is air/gas in the intestinal wall. It is not supposed to be there and can be quite dangerous if it gets to be too much. Grace was not showing any signs of danger at that time, so I brought her home. I was happy to be bringing her home, but I was very fearful once again of what this could possibly develop into and whether I would be able to detect it early enough that it would not cost Grace her life. On Tuesday, we went back for another x-ray which showed no change, so they sent us home once again. Unfortunately, by Saturday Grace started running a high fever of 103.3°, so I rushed her to the University Hospital in Albuquerque. Tylenol brought the fever down and an x-ray showed that the air had improved some, but they decided to admit her because her white blood cell count was high. They did not know the source of the fever but decided to treat the air issue to be safe.

A week later on January 17, we still did not have any answers. All of the tests were coming back negative. Negative tests were good news because of the multiple reasons for infection that we did not want, but it also was bad news, because we did not have the answers we needed to treat the infection. Grace was in the PICU, Pediatric Intensive Care Unit, for the first time. I was getting to know the nurses and doctors really for the first time. I appreciated their thoroughness, their professionalism, and their communication with me, Grace, and each other. I appreciated that they invited me to listen in and participate in their conversations as they did their "rounds" on Grace, always making sure I understood and had my questions answered. I could tell they valued me as a critical team member in Grace's care since I knew her best. The doctors were determined to treat the air in her intestinal wall. I wanted it to be better, but it appeared that it would be a very long and drawn-out process, possibly a couple weeks in the hospital. Grace's fever had not returned and on this morning, she was finally very awake—alert, talking, kicking, smiling, and acting perfectly healthy for her! I was anxious to take her home because the longer the hospital stay, the more likely she would get RSV or pneumonia. I had our prayer warriors praying for the air in her intestinal wall to disappear or lessen so that we could go home. Rich definitely had his hands full juggling work and the other three kids with their busy schedules.

On Tuesday, January 18, Grace was having another good day, almost laughing while she was getting her shaking treatment. The air in her intestinal wall looked better in some places and worse in others. This led the doctor to have a conversation with me that sometimes this air takes weeks and months to go away. She felt the need to start preparing me for the way things might go. If the air did not go away, they would not feel that Grace was stable enough to go home. Therefore, Rich and I would be going against their medical advice if we took her home. The risk could get so bad that the air could perforate the wall, possibly becoming fatal for Grace. She was planning on having a sit-down with all the doctors necessary as well as people from the hospital to discuss our options if the air did not go away in the next day or two. We definitely wanted what was best for Grace, but neither of these options seemed good. We desperately needed God to intervene and to intervene quickly. Every day I was writing on the CaringBridge website asking for more prayers. I knew God could do amazing things; we just had to keep asking. Then, on Wednesday, January 19, the x-ray looked a little better. Our pediatrician stopped by the hospital room to have a long conversation with me about long-term decisions that we would need to have prepared for the meeting on Friday if we decided to take her home against their advice. He also warned me that the meeting could get "contentious." They, of course, were all thinking of the possibilities of it not getting better, and what course would we take in case of emergency or if it continued as it was for too long. Rich had put the day and time of the meeting on his calendar so that he could be there with me. In the meantime, we and our many prayer warriors kept praying that the meeting would not be needed because God would have moved the air out completely.

Praise the Lord: the air was completely gone the very next day, Thursday, the day before the planned meeting. Once again God showed His complete control in the timing of every event in our lives and we were so grateful! Grace was able to be started on Pedialyte through her feeding tube and was able to go home two days later on January 22. As I drove Grace home from the hospital that evening, I reflected back on how God had orchestrated everything once again. If we had not been in on January 10 for that routine test and x-ray, the air may not have been found and could have progressed in a very dangerous way leading to surgery or even losing Grace suddenly. I was amazed at God's goodness! Truly Grace's days were numbered by God, and she would not go home to be with Him in heaven until He chose to take her. The next day was very joyful as we all had a much better night's sleep in our own beds. We were all so happy to have Grace home again. Megan danced with Grace in the kitchen while Grace sat smiling in her chair. What a blessing!

***

We had a couple of very good weeks and then had to return for a follow-up x-ray to make sure the air in the intestinal wall was not back. Unfortunately, it was back, but not too badly. When the doctor saw no other signs of fever, distended stomach, or blood in Grace's stools, we were allowed to go home and just watch her carefully for another week and then we would x-ray her again. The problem with the air being back was that they did not know the reason she had it to begin with. They decided that she must have been constipated. Now they started her on a laxative and she definitely was not constipated. Sometimes I felt like the medical world was a big guessing game, trying to figure out reasons for every issue that came up. Grace's body was definitely a medical mystery to many and a challenging puzzle to be figured out. Just when they got one issue found and fixed, a new one would show up.

About this same time, on February 10, 2011, Rich's dad, Jay, also went in for surgery up in South Dakota. He had been diagnosed with cancer earlier in December. The surgery was exploratory to see if they could slow down the cancer. Unfortunately, they were not able to do anything. They were beginning to make plans to send him home on hospice and we all felt the need to be up in South Dakota with him and the family. On the same day as Jay's surgery, Grace started gagging. She was being given bolus feedings through her feeding tube. This simply means that at certain times of the day, I would pour her formula into her feeding tube for her to digest. After her 2:00 p.m. feeding, she gagged a couple times. Then after her 5:00 p.m. feeding she had lots of gagging. This was enough for me to know that something was not right and I needed to stop her feedings. Instead of giving her an evening feeding at 8:00 p.m., I gave her Pedialyte. Her oxygen level was good that night. She had no fever. When I gave her medications through her feeding tube at 10:00 p.m. she gagged again.

She slept pretty well through the night, but when she woke up at 5:30 a.m. on Friday, February 11, she was grunting and in obvious pain. Her breathing was very rapid, her heart rate was very fast, and her tummy was so hard I could see the veins popping through. I tried to give her medication and Pedialyte through her tube at 6:00 a.m., but she threw it right up. Luckily, Rich was in the habit of taking the kids to school, so I quickly packed up our things and headed for the ER at the children's hospital. I was quite certain this would not be a short stay.

They were very quick to recognize Grace's distress and most likely mine, so she was seen right away. After poking her four times in different veins, they were finally able to get IVs in her left foot and her right arm. She was so tough that she never cried or got upset until the fourth poke. She was so dehydrated that they were unable to get blood for the labs right away. I could not understand how she could be dehydrated when she had been getting normal feedings the day before and Pedialyte, and her body obviously looked like it was storing it all by the hardness of her stomach. Yet here she was dehydrated. They started giving her IV fluids by 8:30 a.m. Her heart rate continued to be high and she was still breathing rapidly and grunting in pain. I did not understand why she was so puffy and was concerned that it was the air in her intestinal wall again. They did finally get labs. By the middle of the night many of her counts were off. She was given magnesium, albumin, and glucose at 3:00 a.m. By 3:30 a.m. her fever was 103.2°. I always had them take rectal temperatures on Grace, because her body did not regulate its temperature well at all and other methods of taking her temperature were never as accurate. I was putting cold wet washcloths all over her trying to get the fever to come down and it didn't seem to be working fast enough. I was relieved when they were able to bring a cooling blanket in to lay over her precious little body. Her fever finally came down to 99° and they were able to take off the cooling blanket at 4:30 a.m.

After a day there, the doctors still did not have many answers. There was still air in Grace's intestinal wall, but it didn't look much different. She was very dehydrated. Her colon was dilated with gas in it and her poor little stomach was hard as a rock. Her whole body was very puffy. She was retaining a lot of the fluids they were flushing through her. Her breathing was still very rapid and they kept increasing her oxygen, hoping to make it easier for her to breathe. The doctors were thinking it was gastroenteritis, a big word for the flu bug. They said her counts were getting better, but her heart was still racing and her respiration rate was still too fast. She was on Tylenol but still in obvious pain any time she had to be moved. She had to be moved every couple of hours so she would not get bed sores. My heart just ached watching her hurt like that. I just held her hand or held her in my arms as still as I could.

The surgeon came in later that day after looking at the x-rays. He told me how very close Grace had been to perforating her colon and needing surgery. He felt they were on the right path but wanted to do more testing to figure out the cause of the air and he anticipated that it would take a week or two to get Grace back on her feeds and home. As of that moment, Grace was not stable enough to do any of that. We had hoped that our whole family could go to see Rich's dad, but we desperately needed God to intervene. We knew God could heal Grace. He had done it many times before.

On February 13, Rich's birthday, Grace was not grunting in pain anymore but she still did not look like herself at all. She had put on seven pounds from all the extra fluid. She was very big, puffy, and heavy. I could definitely tell the weight difference when I held her. They started giving her Lasix to help get rid of some of the fluid. What a balancing act it all was. We went from dehydration and needing fluids to retaining too many fluids and needing Lasix. The chest x-ray from the previous day had shown fluid in her lungs. It was not pneumonia yet but they were starting to talk about the possibility of needing to put a tube in her chest to drain off the fluid. This was not a great option, because any time you put another tube in someone the possibility for infection increases. I had heard that many times in the last few years. Grace already had two IVs in as well as a foley catheter to collect her urine. By this time, I felt very comfortable with the resident doctors and nurses who were taking care of Grace. They consistently had the same doctor for three or four days before the next one came around. There was a total of five doctors that rotated in the PICU. I liked them all and could tell that they had started to know Grace and me well enough that their interest was truly to do what was best for her. So I knew when I asked that day if it was safe for me to leave for a few hours to go be with Rich and the kids for his birthday and they said yes, it really was safe. We were blessed to have a friend from church come sit with Grace while I was gone. She loved and prayed over Grace and diligently kept notes just like I did whenever the nurse or doctor came in to check on her. Another blessing was a wonderful meal and birthday cake prepared by Rich's chef from his hotel and his wife, and also from our church, brought to our door. Members of our life group, ladies from my Bible study, as well as the wonderful people at my husband's hotel really took care of our family through this time. They were all so quick to see the need and come to our aid.

While it was good to see Rich on his birthday and love on my other three kids, my worries were definitely back at the hospital. I know that I sped a bit to get back quickly, and I raced up from the parking garage to get back to Grace's room. I knew she was good or I would have received a call, but what relief came to my heart when I could see with my own eyes my little girl lying in her bed in that PICU room with all of the monitors and tubes attached to her, seeing that she was still safe and well.

That night Grace seemed to do well as they put her on her stomach to sleep. The very next morning, Valentine's Day, they put Grace on her back for her chest x-ray only to have her oxygen level crash down to 48. They moved the oxygen up and her level went up to 82. Then they moved the oxygen up more and put her back on her tummy and it went back up to 95. Her x-ray showed that the fluid had shifted from the right side of the lung to the left. She also now had plural effusion on the left side, which is fluid between the lung and the chest wall. They continued going up on Grace's oxygen levels, both the number of liters per hour as well as the percentage she was receiving. She was getting close to either being intubated once again or putting in a chest tube. The chest tube would give her instant relief, but risk infection, bleeding, and would be very painful.

By Tuesday, February 15, the doctors felt that Grace was getting out of the safe range to intubate her (put her on the ventilator). They said that she was "tricky." As long as she stayed on her tummy, she did well. If moved on to her back or sitting up, her oxygen levels would plummet. If they put the oxygen any higher, it would be very dangerous to intubate her because they would have to take the oxygen off of her to get the tube down her throat. So they brought in their top doctor of the PICU and he did it. The doctor told me that a normal child would have their oxygen levels dropping down low in two to three minutes, but Grace's started dropping in thirty seconds. Her oxygen level went down into the 20s. Her heart rate dropped into the 40s. The doctors and nurses stayed calm and were able to get the tube right in. Having your child intubated is not an easy thing to watch, especially the first couple times, but when you know it is something that will actually bring your child some comfort and rest, it makes more sense and you understand the necessity of it. Once she was intubated, the machine did the work of breathing for Grace. The less work her body had to do to breathe, the more she could rest, allowing her body to work on recovering and to heal faster from the other issues at hand. Knowing and trusting your doctors also helps, and by this time I did trust them. I knew they were human and could still make mistakes, but I also knew they wanted the best for Grace and were fighting with me for her life.

***

By the next day, Grace already looked better. She was still way too heavy, still carrying too much fluid, still receiving Lasix, and her electrolyte counts were constantly changing. Each day they were having to give her something extra, albumin or magnesium. Now that the machine was doing the work breathing for her, she could actually rest, hopefully letting her body heal. She started opening her eyes and moving her hands again even while on sedation and pain medication. The x-ray was already looking better as well. There was still fluid on the lungs, but no sign of pneumonia. It was obvious that we were not all going to be able to go to South Dakota to see Rich's dad, so I consulted with the doctors, and they thought this was the best time for Rich to go. So he packed up himself and the other three children and started the drive. My heart ached that I could not go to support Rich and the kids and see his dad again, but it just was not meant to be this time.

When Rich and the kids headed up north on February 16, my parents got in their car and started heading south to come be with Grace and me. When they got into town they came straight to the hospital. I know it was so hard for them to see Grace in that condition. She did not look good with her stomach all hard and distended, and the tubes and wires all over her precious body. I could see the pain and concern in their eyes as they walked into the room and assessed the situation. They both walked over to Grace, held her hand, stroked her hair gently, gave her kisses and words of love. I know they missed her terribly when we moved, and although they were very supportive when we moved away from Omaha, their hearts' desire would have been to enjoy seeing her and my other kids much more often than they were now able. My dad always sang "Jesus Loves Me" to Gracie and held her as much as possible whenever he saw her. Now she was in such pain every time she was touched or moved that we could only take turns standing by her bedside, holding her hand, and touching her. He did still sing softly to her, though.

For the next few days our *Mamasita*, Spanish for "Little Mama," which some of the nurses fondly called Grace, seemed to be doing better with her breathing. They were able to lower the settings of the ventilator. Unfortunately, the gas in Grace's colon continued to get worse each day. When we had first arrived at the hospital, they put Grace on a broad-spectrum antibiotic. After a few days, they switched it to a more specific antibiotic that would treat her UTI properly. Apparently the first antibiotic was treating something they did not know was there, because as soon as they switched, Grace started running a fever again and her white blood cell count went up again indicating more infection. They continued running tests for the next couple days trying to find out where the infection was. This really didn't surprise me too much. Rarely did we end up in a hospital stay with Grace ever having just one infection. Grace had always managed to keep the nurses hopping and the doctors guessing, because her body was such a mystery in the way that it worked with all of the different anomalies.

While Grace's pneumatosis was still gone, they did finally find an infection called pseudomonas. This is an infection that people can get if they already have a weakened immune system because of another illness or condition. They are automatically at a higher risk for getting an infection and this is especially true for people hospitalized for an extended period of time. This definitely fit Grace's description. They started yet another antibiotic for Grace. The doctors continued planning to run some test on Grace's colon, but she was still in too much pain so they did not do it right away. I could see the pain on her face. It was so hard to see her hurting like that.

I was very relieved when Rich and the kids got back home on February 20. I knew it had been very hard for them to say their goodbyes and leave his dad in that condition, but with Grace's condition being so unpredictable, it was good to have them back. My parents stayed a while longer to continue helping. Dad stayed with me at the hospital a lot. Mom did so much, helping everyone at the house with laundry, cooking, and cleaning, and then coming up to see Grace while the kids were at school. The ladies from the church were also bringing meals to the house.

Grace was able to come off the ventilator by February 20. Her lungs looked better, her pneumatosis was still gone, but by the next day her abdomen was harder and bigger. Grace was off the ventilator but still working so hard to breathe. Her white blood cell count was up even higher to 156,000 which was screaming INFECTION to us all. Why were these antibiotics not taking care of it? Ultrasounds and x-rays were not showing anything new. Grace had not had a bowel movement for eleven days so they did an enema. I didn't think too much of it since she had not been on her regular feedings for a few days. She was just receiving IV fluids and TPN, which is a method of feeding that bypasses the gastrointestinal tract. The fluids are given into a vein to provide most of the nutrients that the body needs.

The enema did not provide any real relief. Grace was now on three heavy-hitting antibiotics and her white blood cell count was up to 159,000. She had a fever again in the night and pain all day. The surgeon consultation on February 22 resulted in a CT scan later that afternoon. They decided that Grace's colon was way too large and that she needed surgery immediately. The surgeon explained that the possible reasons for the enlarged colon were either Hirschsprung's disease or that possibly her C-Diff had gone toxic, causing the colon to get bigger.

We did not have much time before they took Grace into surgery that evening at 7:30 p.m. The surgery ended up being damage control. Her colon had already perforated. They took out the parts of the colon that were dead, leaving the parts that were healthy, and then cleaned out the waste from her body as best as they could. There were two good parts of colon left that they stapled together and then they left her stomach open since she was so sick. It was open a few inches. I never would have dreamed three years before that I could handle looking at something so graphic, especially on my own baby, but God sustained me and even gave me the desire to see exactly what was done. I wanted to understand what was going on with that little body as best as I could. The plan was to go back into surgery in two days to reconnect her colon, clean her out again, and decide if they needed to give her a stoma bag for her bowel movements, but first we need-ed Grace to make it through the night. Grace was in a very critical state. That night they were giving her units of blood, blood thinners to prevent clotting, TPN, three antibiotics, lipids, dopamine and epi-nephrine to help her blood pressure, and Versed and fentanyl for her pain. Just because she was out of surgery did not mean she was safe and going to make it. Her infectious fever had obviously been from the perforated colon with that waste spreading through her body. She was in toxic shock and very critical. We had known that she had some malrotation of her intestines and now they told us that it should have been fixed earlier so that this would not have happened. The doctors think that they possibly would rotate and then rotate back. When they were rotated the pneumatosis would occur and then they eventually got stuck when the colon got so bad. But there was no point in fixating on what should have or could have been done. This was where we were. That night Grace was still wide awake at midnight. She was not getting much sedation or pain medication because her blood pressure had been so low. She was struggling through the night, but eventually got a little rest. I fell asleep at 3:15 a.m. and woke up at 6:30 a.m. to Grace having a cooling blanket on again. Her temperature had spiked up to 104° while I dozed off. They were able to bring it down eventually.

By the afternoon of February 23, Grace's fever had spiked again to 106.2° with a heart rate of 213. They were having a difficult time with her blood pressure, which kept dropping too low in the night. She couldn't have Tylenol because they couldn't put anything into her feeding tube. They used the cooling blanket as well as ice packs on the IV fluids, and ice packs and wet cloths on her tummy and forehead. She was swelling up and it took a long time for the fever to come down. Finally, at 3:00 p.m. her fever came down to 102°. I hated seeing Grace suffer so much and was simply asking people to pray God's best for her. I selfishly wanted healing so that we could take her home, but if heaven was God's best plan for Grace this time, then that was what I wanted.

***

Rich's dad was also continuing to decline. He never was well enough to go home from the hospital. I know it was very difficult for Rich to be torn between his dad and his baby girl. I appreciated so much that he was with me. We just had to trust that God was sufficient in taking care of the needs of his dad and the family up in South Dakota just as He was for us there in Albuquerque.

On that long afternoon of February 23 I couldn't keep my eyes open any longer, so I took a nap at 3:30 and when I woke up at 5:30, I was so grateful to hear that Grace's fever was gone! We had brought the kids up to see her as the doctors thought it would be good for them to see her just in case she did not make it. Since Rich was the one at home, he was the one to inform the kids of why they were coming to visit Grace. This was day 13 of her hospital stay so they knew it was a serious one. We were blessed that day to love on Grace and be with her even in such a critical state. We did not know what tomorrow would hold, but we were thankful that we'd had that day.

Psalm 62:1–2, "My soul finds rest in God alone; my salvation comes from him. He alone is my rock and my salvation; he is my fortress, I will never be shaken."

The doctor decided to postpone the next surgery one more day. He wanted to give Grace a little more time to stabilize and hopefully be more rested for the surgery. Her fever stayed away and her blood pressure was much better. She was able to go off one of her blood pressure medications and the doctors were able to lower the other one. Her heart rate was down to 100 all day! Overall it was a good day, a day that gave me renewed rest, strength, and hope that God's ways were best. He had given Grace the strength to make it through such difficult times so far and He could choose to do it again through the next surgery on the next day. I was reminded of Deuteronomy 33:25b, "And your strength will equal your days." God gives us exactly what we need for each day, not for tomorrow and not for a week from now, but definitely enough for today!

The next day, February 26, brought sunshine to our window and sunshine to my spirit as well. God had continued to help Grace do well through the night. She had no fever; her lungs were pretty clear in spite of the fluid she was retaining throughout her body. Her blood pressure had been good and she was no longer on the medications for it. She had continued to get puffier through the last twenty-four hours, but that was expected. I thought that she was in the best condition possible going into this next surgery. They could not give us a specific surgery time. It would be when they could fit her in. Our surgeon was very caring towards Grace. He came often to check on her and answered all of my many questions. The plan for surgery was to clean the rest of the waste out of Grace's body, possibly doing a rectal biopsy to check for Hirschsprung's disease, placing a stoma with a bag, and assessing the colon when they got in there to decide if it could be repaired or if more needed to come out. He was unsure if they would be able to close her up. It would depend on how swollen her bowel was. Soon after that conversation, they took Grace back for surgery. It was 3:10 p.m. They were done by 4:40 p.m. and I was relieved to see the surgeon because it had taken longer than I expected. They did not repair the colon because it was all still too messy and it would probably leak. He said her week had just been too dangerous and that we could go back in a few months to fix it when she was healthy. They cleaned her out and thought that they were able to get most of it. Then they took out the ileostomy and added a bag. They also took out Grace's caecum, the first section of the large intestine, because it was obviously dead.

The very same day, February 26, we lost Rich's dad to his battle with cancer. The thought of how close we had come to losing Grace just days before and the reality that she was still not safely home was too much to bear. I simply could not let my mind wander to the "what if" place where Grace was concerned. I knew God had a perfect plan, but I was desperately praying that there would not be two funerals in the Lundt family that close together.

Grace continued to run a fever the next couple days after her second surgery. Her electrolytes were off once again and her heart rate was just doing crazy things. It was 135, and then every couple of minutes it would jump up to 230, 250, or even 270. Then it would go back to normal. Her blood pressure would also dip during these fast heart rates. They did an EKG and decided to leave it on for twenty-four hours to monitor her heart. Her fever finally went away on February 28, but they had to start her on a new pain medication. Grace needed yet another unit of blood that helped with her blood pressure, but her heart rate would not go down with the new medication. I had given blood many times before and knew the importance of it, but my little girl getting much-needed blood during this time that was not my type, brought new meaning and importance to the need for people to give. Grace's white blood cell count had been at 57,000 and was finally starting to come down by March 1. Grace had been back on the ventilator since her second surgery and we were finally starting to come down on those numbers as well.

My parents and Rich and the kids all left Albuquerque and headed north for the funeral. I was very grateful for God's timing in everything that had happened. Rich and the kids were able to spend some quality time with his dad two weeks before he passed away. Then they were all with me when Grace was in such a dangerous time with her health. Now that Grace was more stable, they could go focus on his family as they needed to. I desired to be with them, but my place was at the hospital with Grace. I had been with her since day 1, and now on day 20, March 2, the day of my father-in-law's funeral, I was where I needed to be. I wished I could have said good-bye and told Jay how much he'd meant to me and that I loved him, but I do believe he knew. He had always been so good to me, so supportive, and a wonderful father. I was truly blessed to have known him and to have been his daughter-in-law.

After Grace's last surgery on February 26, the surgeon did not close up Grace's wound. The opening in her stomach was about one inch wide and four inches long. I had a difficult time envisioning how a wound this large would close up on its own, but I trusted that the surgeon knew what he was doing. It was not the first part of God's creation of the body that I did not understand and it would not be the last. On March 2, they put a wound vac on Grace's incision. This was supposed to speed up the healing process and also help with the swelling. We continued to pray that Grace would not get any more infections during her hospital stay so we could focus on healing from this and getting home.

On March 4, they tried to extubate Grace (take her off the ventilator). She seemed to handle it well at first, but it was not long before she was working too hard to breathe and her respirations were too fast so they knew they had to put her back on the ventilator. This was discouraging as the doctor told me this would definitely extend Grace's hospital stay. We felt we were making progress towards getting home.

I tried not to get discouraged, but it was difficult. I knew that Rich was doing well with the kids at home, but it was difficult for him to get everything accomplished. I was always trying to find rides for the kids to get over to his hotel after school so he wouldn't miss meetings and valuable work time. We all just wanted to be home together where we belonged.

***

The rest of March seemed to be quite a rollercoaster ride. Just when we thought we were making progress toward getting home, something would get worse. The doctors would make progress getting the fluid off of Grace's lungs with the Lasix, but then her kidney levels would not look good and they would have to take her off the Lasix. To improve one area seemed to counter-attack another part of her body. They would get her back on her feeds of Pedialyte, and then to formula. She would be about halfway to the amount of formula she needed, and then she wouldn't handle her feeds well so they would shut them down again. She continued needing to get units of blood because she was anemic on many days. Her fever came back with a UTI, but then suddenly one day her body's temperature went too low and we started struggling with that.

Due to Grace's long stay, they had to change her IV access multiple times. They always needed more than one, and with the need for TPN they needed to put in a central line. A central line is usually inserted in the chest or arm through the skin into a large vein. It is better able to handle the many medications, fluids, nutrients, or blood products put into it over a long period of time. Grace's sweet little veins had been poked so many times in her short life that they were getting more and more difficult to find because they were so beat up. They would roll away the second the needle came near. On March 11, we were told that since we had been there for a month, we needed to choose a primary PICU pediatrician for Grace. We would start having care conferences with them and they also would assign us some primary nurses, so we would not constantly be getting new nurses. This would be helpful, because while all the doctors were very good, sometimes their plans or reports conflicted with each other. One day we were told we would be there about ten to fourteen more days, and then two days later we were told by a different doctor that it would be another three or four weeks! After being in the hospital for that many days with your little one, even being told three or four more weeks was emotionally hard to take. They were also putting in the central line that day. They were putting this one into the left side of Grace's neck but were having quite a difficult time. They had an ultrasound to help guide them to the vein, when they realized that Grace had yet another anomaly. She had a bilateral superior vena cava, meaning that her veins went into both the right and left atriums of her heart, where most people's veins connect and go into one atrium.

Earlier in the hospital stay we had been struggling with Grace having tachycardiac spells where her heart rate went way too fast. Now on March 17, at a little after noon, Grace stopped breathing and her heart rate went down into the 50s! The nurses came running in and bagged her, giving her the oxygen she needed so badly at the moment. As you can imagine, these were very scary moments. As the mom, I just had to stand back and watch them, hoping and praying that it worked, that she would start breathing again on her own and that her heart rate would go back up.

This was about the time in the stay that the only words that came to my mind were, *Your will, not mine.* Grace's heart rate plunged two more times on that day. These episodes, in which the heart rate goes way too slow, are called bradycardia episodes. They did a CT scan and found three or more abscesses that needed to be drained. Later that afternoon they took Grace to radiology to put drains in each of these abscesses. They were able to get a lot of pus and blood out of them. Grace handled it well and came back to her room with three more tubes coming from her stomach. These were to continue the draining.

When things calmed down, the nurse and the doctor both had conversations with me. The nurse was concerned that Grace was just getting worn out. This had been a long hospital stay, and quite the battle, fighting infection after infection. The doctor was equally concerned that Grace was still taking such dramatic turns for the worse so far into this hospital stay. We had been there for thirty-six days by March 18. They had continued doing trial feedings that always seemed to get stopped. They had been doing "sprints" with Grace on the ventilator. They would turn the ventilator settings down for a couple of hours at a time, requiring Grace's lungs to do the work. They were conditioning her lungs to be able to get off completely, but she was still not off.

Staying in the PICU almost non-stop posed several challenges, the biggest of which was being drawn into discouragement or depression. With the lack of sleep on my part and the lack of steady progress on Grace's, it was difficult for me to stay focused and stay positive. I remember specifically that there were about four days where I flirted with the temptation of anorexia. The days were obviously full and it would be easy to just not go get food. I was already concerned that the diet I kept there, as well as my lack of exercise, would make me gain weight. I didn't totally stop eating, but absolutely was not eating enough. After a few days, I found myself researching anorexia. I was telling myself that it wasn't what I was doing, but then had to read about it to confirm it. I was having these mental arguments with the Lord that it was okay and I had it under control. The truth was that between my marriage crashing and these fearful moments with Grace, I felt like I had no control. I had no control over whether our marriage survived or whether Grace stayed alive. I finally came to my knees with the Lord and confessed my sin to Him. I gave up the right to control those things that were never mine to control. I am a person of habit and realized later that my flirtation with anorexia was my way of trying to keep some control in a life that was very much out of my control.

***

There was a healthier way to deal with it though. I would wake every morning close to the same time, and walk down the hallway to the place where I could shower and get cleaned up for the day. I became quite quick so I would not miss much time in Grace's room. I was always watching for the doctors as they did their rounds. The PICU was in a circle, so I would gauge which direction they were going and how soon before they would be in Grace's room. I would participate in rounds, sometimes adding input and other times just listening, intently taking notes so I could review and compare later to previous days. After rounds when the nurse and CNA came in to give Grace a sponge bath and take her vitals, I would hustle down to a little shop in the first-floor lobby area where you could get food off the grill or just snacks off the shelf. Every morning I would get the same breakfast, a breakfast burrito with strawberry milk. I would take it back up to Grace's room so she would not be alone. At other times during the day if a nurse was in her room or watching from the desk at the window, I would run to a family room where computers were available and update the CaringBridge website. We had many friends and family members who kept up with news of Grace daily and were praying for her often. I kept it as up to date as possible with specifics to pray for. The rest of the day was filled with nurses, doctors, respiratory therapists, specialists, the surgeon, pastors from our church, Child Life specialists, housekeeping lady, ladies from Bible study, Rich almost every day, and the many more who came in for various reasons.

I was not just Grace's mom, but I was her biggest advocate. I knew every medication she was on, every normal and abnormal way her body worked and reacted to different things, every surgery and procedure she had been through, what organs were most at risk, what her facial expressions and sounds meant—her only ways to communicate. If I wasn't there to speak for her, no one would. I had to be her voice. I had to push the call button or call down the hall. I had to make it known that her life had value, that she had a dad and a mom who wanted more time with her to love on her, she had two brothers and a sister at home who could not wait to see her again, to play with her, to hold her. I had to make it known that she was loved and valued, that her life was worth fighting for. I taped a picture of Grace with her brothers and sister to the end of her bed, knowing full well that Grace's blind eyes could not see it, but knowing full well that every person who came in to care for Grace knew she was loved.

During the quiet times, I would do Bible study and we almost always had Christian radio (K-Love) playing in our room. At bedtime, Grace and I would have our quiet time together. I would read her Scripture, sing praise songs, and pray with her. I would continue to tell her nightly what I had told her during her first hospital stay back in Omaha. I would tell her about heaven and the wonderful place that it was because Jesus was there and she would be all healed there. For the first time in all her hospitalizations, I would tell her that if Jesus came for her, to go quickly because these nurses and doctors were really good! I would tell her it was okay for her to go. We would miss her, but we would all be with her in heaven soon! Then I would go lie down on my bed behind hers, pull the blankets up over me, and sing my own version of "There Will Be a Day" by Jeremy Camp. It is a beautiful song about heaven that talks of no more tears, pain, or fears. My version included no more doctors, needles, and pain. Gracie had endured so much of them all.

The truth was that heaven was neither a place to be feared, nor would it be a boring place where we sit on clouds all day singing. God had placed a love for heaven in my soul long before. As a child I had loved singing songs about heaven. My favorite Christian artist group in our early years of marriage was called FFH, which stood for "Far From Home." Much of their music was about heaven and my favorite song of theirs was called "Ready to Fly." My grandmother on my mother's side, Lois Tindall, was the most heaven-minded person I knew. She talked of heaven often and was so looking forward to going and drinking coffee with Jesus. She was truly hoping for Jesus' return when we all would meet Him in the sky! She had given me the book *Heaven* by Randy Alcorn. I wanted to desire heaven as she did, and with all of the thoughts of Grace going there soon, that desire was definitely growing in me again. To be with Jesus, and not have any more physical or emotional pain, sounded incredible to me as I shared Grace's time in the PICU! A popular song, "I Can Only Imagine" by MercyMe, played often on Christian radio, allowing my thoughts to stay focused on how wonderful heaven would truly be.

Our wonderful church was also very heaven-minded. Pastor always said, "There is a heaven and there is a hell, and people are going to one place or the other." He was very good at reminding us to be "others" focused. I needed to keep my eyes off myself. Sitting there in the PICU for all those days and nights, it was impossible not to see others. I rejoiced when the little children were healed and either went up to another floor because they were not critical anymore or, even better, when they got to go home! I cried and mourned when there would be a section of the PICU blocked off while loved ones in tears, sometimes barely able to hold each other up, filed in and out all day long, saying their last good-byes. Then the hour at night came when all was quiet and someone would push a cart with that little lifeless body on it in some form of a gunny sack. I did not like the looks of the bag they put the body in and determined that Grace would not go out in that kind of a bag. I would bring her cozy sleeping bag for that purpose, if and when that day came.

Through the last half of March, Grace's lungs continued to do better. She came off the ventilator finally on March 20. She continued to scare us with the bradycardia episodes and she continued to be in pain. On March 25, they took out three drains from the abscesses, but then put in another two. One night when I had gone home for a few hours, which I only did if someone came to sit with her, I got back to her room and Grace was very upset, crying, and needed to be suctioned. She was running a fever and breathing rapidly. The guilt I had been feeling for being away just compounded. I quickly got the nurse to take Grace's temperature, give her some Tylenol, and get cold, wet rags on her. Soon after that, Grace calmed down. She was very sweet and gave me some smiles. These smiles did not come easily when you were as sick as Grace had been. I felt like God was using her to let me know that it was all okay. Mommy didn't need to feel so guilty and bad. I knew it was important for me to spend time with Rich and the kids, but it was such a struggle feeling guilty that no matter how I tried, no one was getting the attention and love they needed.

***

By the end of March, day 47 in the hospital, Grace was moved out of the PICU. While this was a good sign that she was getting better and getting closer to going home, the medical staff specifically told me their concerns that Grace would need me to be very present on the other floor because the nurses were more spread out with more patients. My other concern was that with the move to another floor would come new doctors and nurses—doctors and nurses who had received the reports but did not know my child.

On April 1, day 50, Grace was doing so well that I was finally able to hold my baby girl without it hurting her to move her. It had been a very *long* time! She fell asleep in my arms right away and I loved holding her for every minute of that nap, even when my arms were weary from her weight. Grace was smiling at everyone who came in! I had not seen her this happy in such a long time and I could not wait to get her home. Our new goal was to get her home by her birthday, April 10! Everyone knew it and were making plans toward it. She got another one of her drains taken out of her abscesses, and only one was left. They continued to change her wound vac and the wound continued to heal and get smaller. I was learning my newest nursing skill—how to take care of the ileostomy bag. I was emptying it and changing it. The excitement was building! We just kept praying that our plan was God's plan. By April 5, Grace was up to full feeds, but she was still on a little oxygen, still had one drain in, and was still on IV antibiotics. Each doctor was letting their opinion be known as to whether they thought she was ready to go home. One day as I was discussing the possibility over Grace's bed, she started laughing! Grace had this breathy laugh that really had no sound. It was so fun to watch because she rarely did it! On this day it was extra special. It was as if she were trying to convince the doctor that she was ready to go home!

Grace did not quite make it home by her birthday. Her birthday was on Sunday, April 10. By Friday the 8th, Grace's CRP (C-reactive protein) level was at .9. The infectious disease doctor said that they wanted her CRP level down to .3 before they would sign off and let her go home. They had been involved in Grace's case ever since the abscesses showed up. On Friday they decided to make Grace the exception to the rule, but they made it clear to us that it was with some risk because the abscesses were not completely gone. Unfortunately, they were not able to get us a wound vac to take home for the weekend. It would not be available until Monday. After sixty days we were finally going home. We were very grateful for God's timing once again. We had just been told that if her stay was much longer, we would have lost Grace's Medicaid and would have had to reapply! I cannot imagine how we would have paid for such large bills without her Medicaid.

This was definitely one of our most difficult hospital stays. Many times we were very unsure if Grace would make it home. To see a child in such pain for so long and to be totally unable to stop it is something no mother ever desires to see. Another aspect that made this stay different as well as difficult was that God started to put different passions into my heart about things that I would like to do. It was like He was giving me new things to do. Normally this is not a bad thing, but as I prayed about these things, my heart knew that they were things I would never do as long as Grace was alive. It was as if He was preparing my heart for the future, but it was for a future without Gracie. I cried as I prayed about these passions because it tore my heart in two to think that God was possibly preparing me for a future without

Grace. I knew that the day would come, most likely sooner than I wanted, but I was not ready to face those thoughts. Even though I knew they were from God, I felt guilty for even having those thoughts and desires in me. Little did I know that indeed, He was starting to prepare me for the day that was less than a year away.

We had a list of things that needed to be accomplished before Grace was officially discharged:

1. All medications and IV antibiotics to be available.

2. The home-going wound vac machine to get to the hospital, as well as the PICC line supplies.

3. Grace's wound vac dressing and ileostomy bag to be changed.

4. Getting the necessary oxygen supplies for use at home.

5. All follow-up appointments with the many doctors to be made.

6. An Epogen shot to be available at home.

7. All the extra supplies to be ordered from the medical supply company.

8. The discharge papers to be completed, very time consuming.

9. And finally, I had to have the ability to do all of these new tasks to care for Grace's new needs. She would be going home on oxygen, receiving antibiotics through the PICC line, needing wound care for the hole that was still in her stomach, and needing care of the ileostomy bag. I had done the oxygen and PICC line before, but never the wound care and the ileostomy bag.

Psalm 108:3–5, "I will praise you, O LORD, among the nations; I will sing of you among the peoples. For great is your love, higher than the heavens; your faithfulness reaches to the skies. Be exalted, O God, above the heavens, and let your glory be over all the earth."

The anticipation of getting our precious girl home was very great for all of us. As we loaded Grace into her kid-kart and loaded our belongings and supplies onto the cart to be wheeled downstairs with the nurse, I felt like I could bounce off the walls with joy! The nurse waited with Grace in the lobby while I ran to the parking garage to get my van and drive it down to where I could pick her up. We gently loaded Grace in the van, being careful not to disturb any of the many things now attached to her little body. We loaded our belongings in the back of the van and started our drive home. We arrived home at 5:30 p.m. and were greeted by three very happy children and a very happy daddy! We were all so happy to be together again that no one seemed bothered by Grace's new needs and attachments.

***

The first couple days and nights at home were difficult. Grace had been lying in a hospital bed for eight weeks! She was in a lot of pain whenever she was moved. Once we got her settled, she would calm down. We were doing pain medication around the clock. After a couple of nights, she woke up happy and content, only needing the pain medicine once the next day. Her wound was closing up quickly. I still had to take her in to the clinic to get her wound vac changed every Monday, Wednesday, and Friday. We were quite busy with that plus other appointments and CT scans on Tuesday. Grace seemed to be getting better. The abscesses were substantially better and she was almost done with the antibiotic. We were blessed to have a night nurse four nights a week temporarily, which helped me immensely.

All seemed to be going well until the end of April when Grace seemed as if she was in pain again. Her pain tolerance was very high. She usually never cried during IV sticks until the third or fourth stick, and even then, it was just a whimper. Now she was crying, so I knew something was not right and was very concerned. By the beginning of May, Grace's CRP count was low enough to take her off her IV antibiotics and take out her PICC line! In spite of all this good, her seizures had started to increase. She was now up to twenty-nine in one day. By the next week she was having forty-one seizures in a day. We still had not figured out the source of Grace's pain. We were speculating about everything. We could not move her at all for diaper changes or cathing, nor move her from chair to bed or bed to person without causing pain.

Then God revealed the source of Grace's pain to Rich. He noticed that her left knee and thigh were swollen. So I took Grace to the doctor and they did an x-ray. The x-ray showed that Grace had a broken leg. Her femur was broken right above her knee. The doctor said that it had already started to heal so he thought our time frame of ten days ago was probably accurate for thinking of when it happened. I felt awful. I wasn't even sure I knew how it happened although I had my suspicions. The doctor was very sweet. He told me that we probably didn't even do anything wrong. He said that kids like Grace who are immobile have very fragile bones and he has seen them break just putting them into the bathtub. He put an immobilizing brace on Grace's leg. I think that the nurses and I had been so focused on Grace's tummy issues that we hadn't even noticed her leg. We were so thankful that God revealed it to Rich and now it would be able to heal properly and we could help control her pain. It was a good reminder to me that, in my inadequacy, God is very adequate.

2 Corinthians 3:5, "Not that we are competent in ourselves to claim anything for ourselves, but our competence comes from God."

Just a few days after that doctor's appointment, Grace was feeling much better. Her swelling was way down. She was once again giving lots of smiles and played a fun little kissing game with me. She would turn her head to me to give me kisses and then turn away. Then she would quickly turn back to give me more! This game went on for a long time because we were both enjoying it so much and she had not been feeling good enough to do anything fun like that for a long time. Our nurse was so tickled and surprised to see Grace's personality come out. She had not been with us long enough to see that side of her.

Our summer with Grace was very uneventful. She had a UTI and struggled with a cold and cough. We were able to get her swimming again toward the end of June. She had not been in a pool for so long that she immediately curled up in a little ball in my arms, but it didn't take long before she stretched out her legs and arms and relaxed in her lifejacket in my arms and each of her siblings', as they took turns floating her around the pool on her back. Grace was able to spend lots of time with our family at the ball games and tournaments. Occasionally, when it was too windy or hot, she would stay home with Eric or Ethan. They were both well trained in caring for her. They were even able to do her feedings through her feeding tube. Megan was also well trained in many of Grace's needs. After we finished using the wound vac with the hole in Grace's stomach, we had to fill the hole with a long strip of gauze that would soak up the moisture and continue closing up the hole. The boys didn't like looking at the hole in Grace's stomach, but Megan was all in. She would help me pull the wet strip out and put the dry one in.

There were two different softball tournaments that I took Megan to out of town when Grace, who was also with us, ended up in the emergency room. Both times were over feeding tube issues that were not normal for us. I never really understood why God allowed those to happen, but I came to realize that it was most likely not for Grace and me, but for whoever was working in the ERs on those nights. I would have to share all of Grace's very lengthy medical history and woven into all of her history was miracle after miracle. I figured that either those workers needed to see Grace to see that her life did matter or maybe they just needed to hear me testify to how God was so faithful and good to always take care of her. Whatever the purpose, I hope God was glorified. Many times in our lives we end up in places we don't want to be in or may not think are necessary places for us to be in, but we need to remember every minute of every day is orchestrated by God. He places us with certain people at certain times and He has a purpose for it all. It may very likely not be about us! We just have to walk in the Spirit being led by Him and being obedient to His calling.

Fall came with the usual changes in the weather, activities, sights, and smells along with cooler, crisper weather for football season. Rich especially loved the smell of the wood-burning chimineas in the neighborhood. I loved seeing the many hot air balloons that were in the sky every morning. The number of balloons increased as Albuquerque's hot air balloon fiesta approached. We were grateful that Rich's brother and his family would soon be visiting. Visits from family were few and far between. We had many plans of eating at our favorite restaurants, hiking, and going to the hot air balloon fiesta. A special treat would be a Casting Crowns concert for Rich and I and his brother and his wife!

The concert was a very special night of worship for us. The song "Already There" by Casting Crowns truly hit home. What a great comfort this song was, reminding me that in all the difficult moments in the past few years, whether big or small, God was already there. The truth was becoming more clear to me each year and with each hospitalization that my world was completely out of my control. As much as I tried to have routines and schedules and make sure I did all that I could to keep everyone in my family healthy, I really had no control. Time and again, God proved that He was already there and in complete control. He was there before we received the diagnosis. He was there before Grace aspirated and got pneumonia. He was there before each surgery happened. He was there before the heartbreak, pain, and sorrow of our marriage crashing. He was there before I found Grace face down in her bed without breath. He was there before Grace's colon perforated and she went into toxic shock. He was already there before each tragic event happened, which meant that He was in control of the outcome. Even now, as I was still unsure of Grace's future, He was already there. I did not have to have all the answers because He did. I did not have to know the who, what, when, where, and why, because He did. I knew He loved me and that His plans for me and for Grace were good so I could definitely trust Him. He had proven that to me over and over.

Romans 8:28–29, "And we know that in all things God works for the good of those who love him, who have been called according to his purpose. For those God foreknew he also predestined to be conformed to the likeness of his Son, that he might be the firstborn among brothers."

***

Most of fall was relatively calm. Grace was back to getting physical therapy and even received some swim therapy! She was getting more talkative once again and letting us know her desires, likes, and dislikes. Our wonderful nurse taught her how to do high fives, although Grace didn't do them with just anyone.

She had a biopsy done in September to find out if she had Hirschsprung's disease and it came back negative! While doing that, the doctor found an anal duplication cyst and took a picture of it on his phone that he was quite anxious to show me and others. Apparently, it was quite rare. I was not all that surprised as Grace had many rare things going on with her body. He said it was nothing to be concerned about, but it could be removed at her next surgery if we wanted.

Her next and hopefully final surgery was scheduled for October 18. This would be a reversal of her ileostomy. One surgeon would be putting her ileum back inside, which meant that we would no longer need the bag outside of her body for her bowel movements. Then another surgeon would step in and wrap Grace's ureter in muscle to stop the reflux that Grace had from her bladder to the kidneys. This would protect her kidneys. I was thankful they were willing to do the surgery together. Fewer surgeries, fewer hospital stays! Unfortunately, Grace got an ear infection and a UTI a couple weeks before the surgery was to happen so it was postponed to October 25. One antibiotic covered the ear infection but we would have to go into the hospital early to receive the IV antibiotic that was needed to take care of her UTI.

On Monday, October 24, I loaded Grace and all of our hospital stay necessities into the van and headed to UNM hospital. We were all checked in to our room with our beautiful mountain views. We were grateful that the nurse got Grace's IV in with just one poke this time, another blessing! With the last one fresh in their memories, the kids were all quite anxious about another hospital stay. Megan was especially upset because she had been busy with volleyball and basketball practices and had not been able to spend as much time with Grace as she wanted. She woke early that Monday and got to cuddle Grace before we all had to leave.

I wish I could say that this hospitalization went smoothly, but it seemed to have its ups and downs once again. The surgery went well, but they had to x-ray Grace at the end to make sure the missing needle in their needle count was not in her! Definitely not what a mom wants to hear after surgery. Then the very next day Grace's blood pressure was not good so they had to pump her full of fluids. This improved her blood pressure, but then Grace was not peeing enough. She was starting to swell up again. Then, like a runaway train, other things start going wrong. Grace started having trouble breathing, so they had to start her on oxygen once again because her body was retaining the fluid and it was settling in her lungs. When our very familiar and friendly surgeon came by to check on her, I just had to laugh when he said, "You gotta swell to get well." I was hoping that was true. Then as he walked out the door, he told the other doctor working in the PICU to "fix her." I knew they both loved my little girl.

By the morning of October 27, Grace was looking better. She was opening her eyes again since their swelling had gone down. She was even chatting with me and giving me kisses and high fives! Unfortunately, by the end of the day her breathing became much more rapid and shallow. They had to increase her oxygen levels. Her chest x-ray showed that the upper right lobe and lower left lobe in her lungs were starting to collapse.

On October 28, Grace still had not pooped so everyone was praying for the basics as I called them, pee, poop, and breathing. Three very necessary parts of life that most of us take for granted. They were starting to have concern about IV access again as all of Grace's IVs were not working and they needed to draw blood. They poked her six times and fished around for a vein with no luck. Grace's veins were very worn and, with her puffiness, finding a usable vein was very difficult even with the ultrasound. Finally, they decided to give Grace a break from trying. Later, a new nurse came on her shift and was able to get one of Grace's lines working again. Then we had a few praises that evening when Grace's heart rate and respiratory rate came down to much better numbers, and she pooped! Megan had been texting me and texting me asking if Grace had pooped. Even at the age of ten, Megan knew the necessary things that needed to happen for Grace to get to come home. I was so thankful when I could finally answer yes to Megan's texts!

We had come to learn by now that a day with Grace and a day with God can change dramatically for the better or worse. We never started packing for home too early, and this was the case once again. On October 29, we nearly lost Grace again. The doctors became concerned once more about the need for IV access. Grace's potassium was low and they were not able to put the amount needed in the small IV. So they planned to sedate Grace and put a central line in her femoral artery which was in her groin. We had done this before in a previous stay with no issues. The procedure began with a new resident whom we had never had before. This time, however, the procedure took a long time. The sedation was not very effective as Grace kept moving about. Due to the sedation and her low potassium levels, Grace's heart activity started dropping and her oxygen levels were also dropping. We were approaching the hour mark of working on this, and the doctor doing the procedure was trying to decide if they should stop working on the line so they could intubate Grace (put her back on the ventilator). The oxygen was of great concern, but so was the line to get the potassium and meds needed to help her heart.

I was so weary and the longer the procedure took, the more difficulty I had staying awake. But when I heard the word "intubate," I awoke quickly. At about the same time, the doctor doing the procedure was feeling light-headed and needed to step back. She said to the nurse to call two other doctors and the anesthesiologist. Soon after that she stepped out into the hallway and passed out! Luckily, she landed on a chair and into the arms of a few of the staff around. At the same moment I saw that happen, I saw the nurse start bagging Grace, which meant that Grace was not breathing enough on her own. Everyone else had run from the room to help the doctor. In my panic, I asked what I could do. The nurse very calmly told me not to panic. The other anesthesiologist came in about four minutes. The nurse was still helping Grace breathe with the bag. I stepped out of the room and heard the doctor tell the charge nurse to call the social worker. This was not my first rodeo! I had done this a few times before. The social worker was for me.

The anesthesiologist got Grace intubated very quickly. The social worker arrived and I asked her, "They would tell me if I needed my husband here, right?" So she went to ask the question. The charge nurse came to tell me that Grace's respiratory status was better, but if they did not get a line in very soon, her heart could code. So I quickly called Rich. Thankfully he was working at the hotel and not too far away, and he got to the hospital quickly. I made a few calls to get people praying quickly. I was so thankful for those who prayed and, without needing all the details, made calls quickly for more prayer. After the intubation, the doctor who had passed out was back in the room. They gave Grace some sedation and heart medications straight into her bone. This is usually just done in emergency situations, which is what this had become. Then the doctor was able to put in the central line.

Soon after she got that in, I saw the director of the PICU, my favorite doctor, come strolling into the PICU. I am sure he was one that had been called in the emergency. Now he walked leisurely in wearing his button-down striped shirt, and his hands in his blue jean pockets. Did he not know what an emergency we had just had? How could he just walk in so calmly? He gave me a nod as he walked past me into Grace's room. He assessed the situation with his eyes, saw that all was well now, and went to talk with the other doctor. As odd as it was to me that he didn't come running in to save the day in the middle of our emergency, what was also odd was the immediate peace that fell over me once I knew he was there. My fears hadn't left me when Grace was intubated or even when the central line was in, but his presence brought me peace. He had been the doctor just several months earlier who had really gained my trust during our long, difficult hospital stay.

How much is that like our Savior? We so often want Him to come running in to save us or to fix the situation immediately, but He already has seen it and knows exactly what has been done and what must still be done in what time frame. He alone can give us peace in whatever emergency we face. That peace comes when we truly put our trust in Him. I don't believe you can have the peace without the trust.

Soon after, the doctor called us into the next room to talk. She apologized for passing out. She reassured us that Grace's heart had never stopped and they never had to do chest compressions. They had run a blood gas test and did not think that Grace's brain, kidneys, or liver had taken a hit from what had happened. We were very thankful for God's watch and care over Grace when all of this happened. After this day, I realized that Grace was getting a bit of a reputation in the PICU. She was well known for nothing being as simple as it seemed it should be. I was starting to hear the words "chaos" and "havoc" tossed around affectionately in regard to Grace! I do know she was definitely keeping everyone on their toes and was becoming quite dear to everyone who set foot anywhere near her room in the PICU.

My update on the CaringBridge website for October 29 read:

Rich and I went to a Casting Crowns concert recently. They talked about the woman at the well in John 4. The woman did not understand that Jesus was the well she needed to draw from. He was the one with everything she needed for life and eternal life! They reminded us that Jesus is our well! He has everything we need! I am so thankful that when you drink from the well daily, He gives all you need—especially on days like today! I hope you have all been to the well today! Don't wait for a day like mine to hit you! Much love to all and thankful for another given day with Grace! Cami.

This hospitalization went on a bit longer than planned as well. Grace needed another blood transfusion, her counts were up and down, her lung x-rays took a while to clear up due to an infection they found in them, her fever kept coming and going. We had now managed to be in the hospital for most of the major holidays including New Years, Valentine's Day, Halloween, Christmas, and her birthday! This stay began on October 24. By November 5 Megan was telling Grace that she needed to be home by the tenth and so that is what the doctors started working toward. This time we actually made it home by the goal!

***

While we did not feel like we had rushed getting Grace home, she did not do as well as we hoped. We had to slow down on her feeds because her stomach seemed to get upset until she had a bowel movement. I thought it may be due to her colon being smaller now. Four days later Grace started having lots of diarrhea and a fever again. So the next day I took her back to the doctor's office. They gave Grace some IV fluids and were possibly going to send us back home until the surgeon came in. He looked at her incision site and when he dug down into it, he found a hole with air and puss coming out. It was infected. Back into the hospital we went. There was no talking the surgeon out of it.

The radiologist found another infected abscess so they put in another drain. They also found Grace had another UTI. We rounded off our holiday stays with Thanksgiving in the hospital. Rich came up to the hospital to have a Thanksgiving meal with me that the hospital had prepared. Then I was able to go home for a couple hours to be with the family. Grace was making progress but the culture from the abscess turned out to be e-coli and Klebsiella pneumoniae. She would need to be on IV antibiotics for the next four to six weeks. She would also need to have the drain in for four weeks. They put in a PICC line in hopes of us handling these issues at home. I had to learn to aspirate and flush the drain as well as pack her incision. The doctor believed there was also a fistula, an abnormal or surgically made passage between an organ and the body surface that can also be caused by an infection. His hope was that as we took care of the abscess and the infection, the fistula would heal itself. Hopefully it would not require yet another surgery.

They were ready to send Grace home by November 25, but they ran into some snags with our insurance and Medicaid and the antibiotic we would be needing at home. So we had to stay for the weekend. I was always trying to figure out God's why. I may not truly know all of it, but a little child came into the PICU Saturday night. God placed her right across the hall from Grace's room. They worked all night on this little girl and her condition was obviously very serious. By Sunday night she went to be with Jesus. Maybe God's reason in having me there was simply to pray for this precious little one and her family. Who is to say that Grace's abscess and infection was not part of God's plan to have us there to pray? God's picture and plan is so much broader than we can see. It would be very easy to stay in my small picture frame of me and my child in our room, but God wants us to look outside of that. We are here for Him and for others too! He orchestrates His great plan and lets us play a tiny part in it. I thank the Lord that even though it hurts my heart sometimes to see these things, He invites me into His bigger plan. Grace was released to go home that next Monday, November 29.

As we were coming to a close on the year 2011, the calendar and the memories that went with that year were not the easiest and best to reflect on. There had been many difficult times, days, weeks, and months. Along with those difficult memories, though, were definitely many moments of God's faithfulness and His goodness. There were also many moments of sorrow and joy! God had shown up on the miraculous days as well as on the most difficult of days. I had learned more in the last twelve months than ever before that each one of my children was a gift from God and that He had a perfect plan for their lives. That did not mean their lives would always be easy or even good. That did not mean that just because Grace had completed her last foreseeable surgery for quite some time, she would be living for many more years now, though I certainly hoped so and I was looking forward to just enjoying life again! The truth was and is that my children were His children, totally and completely His! Just as I could not control whether the boys got the flu—which they did!—I could not control the lives of our family. My job was to be the best wife and mom that God allowed me to be and then to place each one of them in His hands each day. It would not be easy and still is not always easy, but I was learning to say, "She's Yours, Lord, not mine."

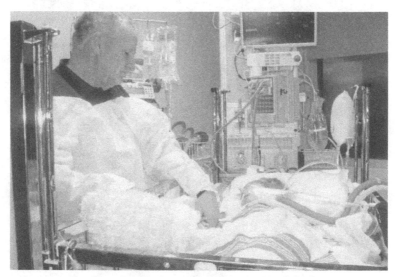

Grandpa Widman with Grace in hospital

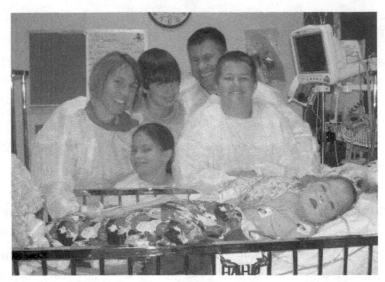

Hospital Family Picture - all in yellow gowns

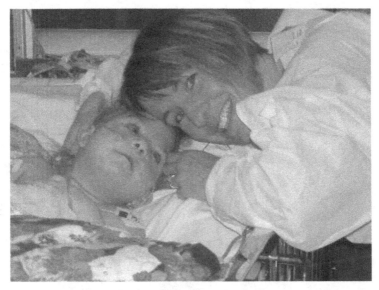

Cami and Grace at hospital

9

Your Will, Not Mine

December 2011 was a good month for the Lundt family. Grace still had her PICC line in her chest where I gave her the IV antibiotics she needed as well as the drain from her abscess. She was still having some pain that we found out was kidney stones. The hospital team continued having us come in for different tests to monitor the abscesses. Regardless of all of these potentially negative things, Grace was home and happy! I was home! Remember how it is all about perspective? Grace was very talkative and I think this was one way she showed us that she was glad to be home.

Megan was now ten years old and she decided to take some gifts up to the PICU at the hospital where Grace had spent so much time. She wanted to make sure those kids up there had a good Christmas. Megan loved Webkinz! These were stuffed animals that had an online code to use on a Webkinz site where you could enter your stuffed animal, pretend-buy them things and play games with them on the computer. So she decided to try earning money by cleaning, baking, and doing supervised babysitting. Then she would be able to buy many Webkinz. She was also given donations to add to her supply. It was a fun project for her to do that month. We enlisted Eric and Ethan to help in transporting all of the Webkinz to the hospital on December 21. Megan was able to take 77 Webkinz gifts up to the hospital that year!

On December 21, the home health nurse was able to pull out the drain for the abscess as well as the PICC line. All of Grace's tests, scans, and ultrasounds came back looking good. Unfortunately, Grace had kidney stones so that was one source of her pain. We were thankful to have all of those things finished so that we could travel to Dallas as a family and spend Christmas with the Lundt family. We celebrated Christmas at Rich's brother's house. It seemed to be a bit easier to celebrate there since it was the family's first Christmas without Rich's dad. We had a very nice Christmas, although I always felt guilty that we didn't get the kids up to my family also that Christmas. I was always worried that each holiday would be Grace's last, and I did the best I could to let all the family see her as much as possible on those special days. After Grace's tough year and the fact that she was still in pain, it just was not smart to be doing two big trips so far away from home, our hospital, and favorite doctors. Sometimes, as the parent/caregiver, you have to make decisions that may not be the best wishes of others around you, but you have to do what is best for your family as well as the medically fragile child in your care.

January seemed to go by quickly as well. Grace continued to be in pain for much of the month, but it seemed to be whenever we moved her and also when she was having a bowel movement. Once again God enabled us to figure out what was causing her pain. One day I had a couple girlfriends over for lunch. One of them had a little guy who was struggling with constipation and diarrhea. He was in pain every time he went to the bathroom. She took him to the doctor and insisted that they test him for perianal strep and, sure enough, he had it. While I was holding him, he had a BM and it seemed crazy to me that it smelled exactly like my Grace's BM's would smell. They were not on the same diet. I took Grace to the doctor the next day. They did not want to test her for perianal strep since she was not showing any symptoms, but they appeased me. Grace had perianal strep! It is caused by the same bacteria that causes strep throat and is very painful. We were so thankful to get her on an antibiotic, hoping now that her pain would go away. Never doubt that God can and will work through you to help another if you are walking with Him.

Unfortunately, the pain did not go away and we had to go in the next day, January 23, for another CT scan. I requested we have someone really good come do her IV so they sent someone from the PICU. It never hurts to ask! That nurse only took two pokes! I suggested we leave the IV in just in case we had to come back if the results were not what we wanted them to be. Notice that I was the advocate all the time, not just during hospital stays. Soon after we got home from the CT scan at 1:00 p.m. that day, we received the call from the doctor's office. The kidney stones looked significantly smaller, but the pneumatosis was back. I needed to take Grace back to the hospital to be admitted so that she could receive IV antibiotics. The doctors made it clear that Grace was not in imminent danger, but they would be x-raying her often to see what direction this pneumatosis was going to go. Three days later the pneumatosis was gone and Grace finally seemed to be pain free for the first time in a long time. She was kicking and moving around! However, this was the exact path her body took last year when they allowed us to go home, only to return later when the pneumatosis had come back with a vengeance, perforating her colon. With her history, they were not going to be so quick to send us home this time. They still had absolutely no idea why this pneumatosis kept coming and going.

They did keep Grace in the hospital for a while as they continued testing and trying to figure out the pneumatosis mystery. I was trying to figure it out as well. I had three dear friends come sit with Grace at different times so I could go to my children's basketball games and to church. During my time at church, God just sweetly reassured me that we don't have to have all the answers when it came to Grace. God had all the answers! He intricately made her and had complete power to heal her. We just needed to continue to rest in Him.

***

They did find some other issues with Grace while we were there. They could not put in another PICC line because they discovered the veins in Grace's shoulders had reproduced into so many little veins that it was almost impossible to get a line in through there. They put in a tunneled central line, which would go straight into her chest instead. It could potentially stay in there for up to a year, though we hoped we would not need it for so long. They also found her pituitary gland to be underdeveloped. This would lengthen our stay as they would have to do some more intense tests involving no feeding, water, dehydration, and lots of blood draws. I did not want to put Grace through these tests, but it was needed in order to get her home. We needed Grace to pee the correct amount according to what she was given, and not too much. The tests showed her urine output was the right amount, and we took Grace home once again on February 5, 2012.

Grace's pain seemed to last for a few days but got better. It finally seemed like we were getting back into our stride at home again, back to normal. The nurse came on her scheduled days and we were just enjoying life again. We were going back to the hospital for x-rays weekly to make sure the pneumatosis stayed away and thankfully it did! I was starting to dream again about all the possibilities for Grace. I would feed her some bites of blueberry yogurt and work with her on sitting up. She was getting stronger, holding her head up better again, and seemed like she was eager to learn new things.

We were all back at church together again and we loved it! Grace would come to the big service with us. On February 19 the worship team led us in singing a new song, "Great I Am" by Phillips, Craig, and Dean. Ethan leaned over and whispered in my ear that it was an awesome song that they had sung in the youth group the previous week. Rich and I instantly fell in love with this new praise song and Rich added it to our playlist as he so often did when he heard a song that touched us or that we just liked. We did not realize how instrumental the perfect timing of this song would soon be.

On the very next Thursday night, February 23, Rich and I were excited to go to another Christian concert. MercyMe gave a great concert. It was an incredible night of worshipping together with Rich! Nights like these drew us closer to God and closer to each other. I knew many of their songs but not all of them. A very powerful song that touched me was "The Hurt and the Healer."

I stood there that night in that dark auditorium with tears in my eyes and my hands lifted high, singing that song in praise and feeling astonished by the words. I felt like I understood them too well. I could still feel the sting of our marriage crashing where the hurt of it all definitely collided with the healer. Even greater in me, though, was the fear I had been facing daily for the last five years, the fear of Grace's death. This song seemed to lay her life and her future death all open in front of me, as if the writer of the song knew my life and the future to come—right down to the line, "when grace is ushered in for good." I know that the song was referring to the wonderful grace of God, but to me it was also a very literal reference to the time when my dear Grace would be ushered into heaven for good, and all her scars would be understood for her. Mercy would take its place. All our questions would fade away and out of weakness we would bow and Christ would say, "It's over now." Her death would usher her right into glory, into to the arms of my sweet Jesus. There would be no more antibiotics, surgeries, or miraculous recoveries. Her life would be complete here on earth, but it would just be beginning in heaven! But, just as the song said, I truly thought a part of me would die with her. I would need Jesus to take my heart and breathe it back to life, just as He had done after our marriage died. What a powerful song, a heartbreaking, gut-wrenching, soul-searching, and if I allowed, a knee-bending, humbling-myself, submitting-to-my-King's-will, kind of song.

The power of the Holy Spirit to use music to touch your spirit and soul is just like that. It had been for me. Little did I know that in the next thirty-six hours, that song would play out line by line in my life once again.

***

Rich and I returned home that night after the concert to check on all our sweet children sound asleep in their beds. Our night nurse was there to take care of Grace, so Rich and I hurried off to bed so I could still take advantage of a good night's sleep. Morning came with the changing of nurses and Rich dropping the kids off at school and then heading to work himself. I got everyone their breakfast and made sure they had everything to get out the door on time. Then I turned my focus back to Grace and our nurse.

Our wonderful day nurse always took the report from the night nurse or from me. The report from the night before was very good, nothing unusual. The nurse went on to gather Grace's medications to give her. Grace had been good when I checked on her that morning. She usually stayed in bed until the nurse got her out. We did our normal morning routine and then suddenly things changed. Grace started grunting in pain and breathing rapidly. Her complexion quickly became pale and her oxygen levels were dropping. We tried to put our oxygen on her, but there was a leak and it was not working very well. The nurse stayed with Grace while I ran across the street. Our neighbor whom I had not met but just shared a friendly wave with now and then was on oxygen all the time. I knocked on her door frantically and she answered. I explained our situation and asked if she had any extra oxygen that we could use on Grace just to get her to the hospital. It so happened that she had a small portable that she allowed us to borrow. The nurse got Grace on the oxygen quickly and kept her eye on Grace's vitals while I got our belongings together. I thought for sure this was going to be yet another hospital stay and they were rarely short. I picked up Grace as carefully as I could, not knowing the source of her pain, and carried her out to the van and put her in her car seat. Our nurse came along with us to help monitor Grace while I drove. We would have to figure out later how to get her back to our house where her car was. Grace was not stable enough for me to go it alone.

We took Grace to the ER and they whisked her right back when they saw her condition, quickly getting her oxygen regulated better and getting her blood levels and setting up her IV fluids. They were very good. We were quickly escorted back through the halls of the hospital to the very familiar elevator up to our favorite area of the hospital, the PICU. I remember those walks like it was yesterday, the tightness in my chest and the worry and anxiety in my head and heart. Once again we were welcomed by many of our favorite nurses and doctors, which always put many of my anxieties to rest. I was so focused on Grace that I didn't even notice until the nurse mentioned it, that we were in the exact same room that we had been in the year before when Grace's colon perforated and we nearly lost her! One of the nurses came in apologizing, "Sorry, we really didn't want to put you back in this room but it was the only one left." I assured her that she should not worry. I had never been a superstitious person. I didn't believe in good luck or bad luck. I totally believed that God was in control and His hand was always in the biggest to the smallest details of our lives, even our room in the PICU.

The doctors went right to work trying to figure out our little girl once again. Her x-rays of chest and abdomen looked good! There was no pneumonia or pneumatosis! Grace definitely had an infection causing these symptoms, but they were unsure where. Her blood pressure was all over the place and they started treating her for sepsis, which "is a potentially life-threatening complication of an infection. It occurs when chemicals released into the bloodstream to fight the infection trigger inflammatory responses throughout the body. It can progress to septic shock, blood pressure drops dramatically, which may lead to death" (Mayo Clinic Overview). Of course, the doctors did not give me the impression at all that we were in a life-threatening state at the time. I look back on part of my CaringBridge entry for that day and realize how used to these circumstances I had become.

CaringBridge entry for February 24:

Please pray: Wisdom for doctors to figure out and treat correctly whatever is going on in Grace's body.

A short hospital stay.

Protection over Grace from all the RSV and other illnesses that are here.

Rich to be able to juggle the schedules of Eric, Ethan, and Megan.

Thanks so much for your love and support! I just started a Bible study on Jonah—how we handle interruptions (God's Divine Invitations) into our lives! It seems like I have had a lot of practice at this, but we will see what God wants to teach me through this one! Love you all, Cami.

I obviously did not yet know the seriousness of Grace's condition. I assumed this was just going to be another of our countless hospital stays. I even went home for a couple hours in the early evening. Grace was in the hands of our wonderful nurse and I had not planned on a hospital stay, so I ran home to get things in order for Rich and the kids before I returned quickly to the hospital. By late evening Grace had been overloaded with fluids, which caused her lungs to get worse. Then they were having trouble keeping her blood pressure up. The blood pressure medications were not enough so they were pushing more albumin into her, which also made her lungs worse. They put in an arterial line to help get a more accurate and consistent blood pressure. I had seen these doctors and nurses jump through many hoops before trying to figure out the cause of Grace's issues and keep up with the multiple symptoms that they brought on. It often looked like a runaway train that they were desperately trying to stop. They had always had success so I was just able to be present, loving my little girl, keeping updated on her status and all that was being done to her and for her. I had confidence in these people and I was confident in my God! As midnight came and my weariness came over me, I did our normal routine with Grace for the last time, reading Scripture to her, praying over her, giving her my words of love about heaven and our great God. Then I went and laid behind her bed on my bed and sang to her our normal songs ending with "There Will Be a Day." I fell asleep at peace that night, having no idea that Grace's "Day" was upon us.

I fell asleep but was wakened only about an hour later as nurses and doctors came rushing to our room. Grace was crashing, her heart was giving way to the infection. As the team of nurses and doctors got the paddles to give her heart the extra help it needed to keep going, I stood with tears in my eyes. In my tired, sleepless state, the Holy Spirit took over and the only words that kept coming out of my mouth were, "Your will, not mine; Your will, not mine; Your will, not mine." Over and over I said it as they gave Gracie a shot to keep her heart going.

When they had stabilized her, the doctor turned around to me and saw the question written all over my face, *What had just happened?* She started to explain to me that they believed Grace had a UTI, a simple urinary tract infection, that had got into her bloodstream. Grace had gone septic when the infection got into the bloodstream and it was now attacking her heart. She said that I should have Rich come up to the hospital to be with me. So, with a lump in my throat, once again I called Rich in tears telling him that I needed him to come up to the hospital because we may lose our little girl soon. I stood next to Grace, holding her hand and stroking her little body while I waited. Then she started crashing and I had to step back again as they came in to bring her little heart back to life once again. The doctor then explained to me that she had put in an order for the strongest antibiotic that had not yet been used on Grace. Apparently, it was very difficult to get and she wasn't sure if they would get it in time. She explained to me that Grace's infection had just been steps ahead of them all along the way. She said they would make little gains on catching up, but then it would jump ahead further.

They finally did get that antibiotic and started it, but it was not soon enough. Rich got to the hospital at about 3:00 a.m., right after Grace had crashed again. The doctor explained everything to Rich so he knew and understood what was happening with Grace. The doctor said that they could keep doing what they were doing, but Grace's little body and heart were too weak to keep fighting. She said they would keep working on Grace as long as we wanted, but that she thought Grace was not going to make it past this infection. She suggested we get Eric, Ethan, and Megan up to the hospital. At 3:30, Rich got back in his car to go get our children. The shots of medication for her heart seemed to keep Grace stable while he was gone. He arrived back at our PICU room with the kids at 5:00 a.m.

The reddened, tear-streaked eyes told me that Rich had told the kids what was happening. I held each one of them in my arms wanting so much to take away the pain of the moment but totally helpless to actually do it. Each one of the kids took their time at Grace's bedside. I don't know what each of them said to her, but I know that she was very present in that moment that her favorite children were there with her. Rich started playing "The Great I Am" on his phone playlist. He played worship music for the next hour while we all just sat there and took turns loving on Gracie. The kids said their last good-byes to Grace and we hugged them all. Then, at 6:00 a.m. a friend from our life group came up to get the kids and take them home. Eric was an awesome big brother comforting Megan and Ethan on the way home until we got there. Once they were gone, the nurse came in and placed Gracie in my arms and turned the volume on the monitors down. Our praise music was still playing, and it was not even ten minutes after her kiddos were gone that Grace's heart gave out. It was as if Grace had said her good-byes to her sister and brothers she loved so dearly and headed for home. She peacefully went from my arms, with Rich's arms wrapped around the both of us, into the arms of Christ.

***

In the end, once again, God had answered my prayers of the last five years. She went quickly and was not in pain. Our precious little girl who had so many limitations on her body here on earth was now free in heaven with no limitations. My sweet Savior had made her lame body walk, her tongue now could talk, and when He opened her blind eyes, the first person she saw was her sweet Jesus! I imagined that her first day and all to follow were filled with dancing, running, and leaping for joy in His presence! This wonderful heaven that I had learned so much more about and had grown to love and long for so much more in the past five years was now a reality for Grace!

After seeing so many other families go through it in the PICU, I had always wondered what my reaction would be when my little girl passed. God made it clear to me right away that even though I was still holding her body, Grace was not there anymore. I had thought it would be so difficult to leave her there in that hospital, but it wasn't like that for me, because God made it so evident that she had already left. Rich and I knew we had three living children at home who needed us, so we gave our Gracie our final hugs and kisses and placed her back in the hospital bed. It was a comfort to have our favorite nurse be there that morning as I explained to her why we were leaving that colorful little child's sleeping bag that Rich had brought up when he went back home to get the kids. I knew that she would clean Gracie up with such care and gentleness just as she had always cared for her, and we left the hospital. We returned home quite early on that Saturday. Even though there was so much that needed to be accomplished and that did get accomplished, it seemed like we were moving in slow motion. It felt like the whole world had stopped. It did not seem possible that this was our reality. For the first time since April 2007, Grace did not make it home from the hospital. There was no healing this time for her earthly body. There was, however, the complete healing that her body had been yearning for since she was formed in my womb.

Titus 1:2, "A faith and knowledge resting on the hope of eternal life, which God, who does not lie, promised before the beginning of time."

The next week God totally held us up. God's timing was very evident to me. Just as the song "Already There" had expressed, God was so evidently there before it all happened! Only an omniscient, all-knowing God would have the ability to intricately plan and orchestrate our being given those specific songs within the week that Grace was to be called home. They were instrumental in our coping and healing, and we even sang "Great I Am" at her funeral. Our marriage, which was so broken two years before, was strong enough to stand through this storm. I honestly don't think it would have been before. We would not have grieved together and made each other strong when we needed to be. Rich was a rock, the godly leader our family needed him to be through our loss. He was instrumental in making sure our time of worship in Grace's death and the time to follow was pointed to Christ.

The year before, when we almost lost Grace, my parents were in the process of buying cemetery plots for themselves in a country cemetery close to the family farm. At that time, we asked them to get an extra one in case we ever needed it for Grace. As much as we loved Albuquerque, I did not want to bury my baby girl in the desert. Also, with our track record of moving, we never knew how long we would be there. We knew that there would always be family up in Iowa to go visit. So here we were a year later, packing up our family and heading to Iowa. Being so close to Omaha where Grace was born felt like we were taking our baby girl back home. God strengthened us with the many friends and family who came to Grace's funeral. Just as God had strengthened me to praise Him for her life in front of that ladies group when I was pregnant with Grace, He strengthened me once again to praise Him for her life at the funeral. That was, after all, what He had called me to do from the moment we got her diagnosis.

God blessed me with one other very special song from that Casting Crowns concert back in the fall. "Wedding Day" took on new meaning now as I played it, giving me such a perfect picture of Grace entering heaven. I love the picture of this grand entrance into heaven, being led by the hand of Jesus wearing white because we are finally free of our sinful earthly bodies. Every tear is wiped away and we will forever reign with Christ! That is what God made us for. That is what He made Grace for.

As grand as our plans for our own life and the lives around us may be, they are nothing compared to God's plans. The sooner we get in line with His plan, submitting to His perfect will, the better off we will be! Even though I had given Grace to God over and over from the day she was born, it wasn't until almost five years later that I was finally able to say, "Your will, not mine." I am so thankful for God's patience in waiting for me to get my heart where it needed to be. Yes, I was always aware that I was walking Gracie home to her heavenly home with her Savior. Honestly, I just always wanted it to be my way and my time, but I always knew there never would have been a right time in my playbook! The story would have gone on and on and on. Once I sat back and took an honest look at the story line God had written out, I could see that His ways were best. They didn't seem best for me, necessarily, because I see things through my sinful selfish lenses. They definitely were for Grace's best—no more sickness, anomalies, suffering, and pain. She would be eternally healed!

We cannot have all the answers to our questions, but if we are open to listening to the Holy Spirit, He will reveal some of those things for us to see. If we keep our eyes open, He shows His presence and His faithfulness all along the way. There are miracles to be seen! There are blessings to be thankful for in this journey. Whether you are in the season of your life right now of "walking someone home'" or if your season is to come, please know that God will equip you with everything you need to do it and to do it with grace, praising Him along the way! Yes, there will be days of pain, struggle, and heartache, but keep your eyes on the prize that we are running for! After all, isn't it our goal to walk each of our loved ones home to Jesus? Whether they are having health issues now in this present time or are perfectly healthy, we are walking/running this race together, and it is worth every minute we are allowed to do it, whether five minutes or five years! With God on our side, we can accomplish much!

1 Corinthians 9:24, "Do you not know that in a race all the runners run, but only one gets the prize? Run in such a way as to get the prize."

Philippians 3:14, "I press on toward the goal to win the prize for which God has called me heavenward in Christ Jesus."

Matthew 5:16, "In the same way, let your light shine before men, that they may see your good deeds and praise your Father in heaven."

I praise God for the blessing of having Grace in my life. If I had the choice to do it all over again or not, I would do it all again in a heartbeat. Pastor Todd Cook at Sagebrush Church in Albuquerque, New Mexico, said that you are always either going into a storm, are presently in a storm, or are coming out of a storm. It is a part of life. God never promised the believer an easy life.

John 16:33, "I have told you these things, so that in me you may have peace. In this world you will have trouble. But take heart! I have overcome the world."

He has promised that He would always be with us.

Joshua 1:9, "Have I not commanded you? Be strong and courageous. Do not be terrified; do not be discouraged, for the Lord your God will be with you wherever you go."

If He has called you to do it, He will be faithful to help you through it.

2 Thessalonians 3:3, "But the Lord is faithful, and he will strengthen and protect you from the evil one."

1 Thessalonians 5:24, "The one who calls you is faithful, and he will do it."

Be encouraged today that you are able to do what God has called you to do if you are His child! If you do not have a personal relationship with Christ, I would encourage you to find someone who can introduce you to Him or just get a Bible and start reading in the book of Luke. He will give you joy and the ability to praise Him through it! You will be blessed and forever changed for the better!

Family picture at Balloon Festival, October 2011

Family picture, taken 2021

Resources:

SOFT - Support Organization For Trisomy
https://trisomy.org

Now I Lay Me Down To Sleep
https://www.nowilaymedowntosleep.org

Joni & Friends Family Retreats - offer a unique setting where the love of Christ surrounds families that are living with the spiritual, emotional, and financial challenges of disability.
https://www.joniandfriends.org

Walking Her Home support through encouragement and prayer
www.walkingherhome.org